A Lifetime for Hungary

Andris J. Kursietis

A Lifetime for Hungary

by

Jenő halmaji Bor

Lieutenant-Field Marshal of the Royal Hungarian Army

Uitgeverij Aspekt

A LIFETIME FOR HUNGARY
© Andris J. Kursietis
© 2014 Uitgeverij ASPEKT / *2e druk*
Amersfoortsestraat 27, 3769 AD Soesterberg, Nederland
info@uitgeverijaspekt.nl-http://www.uitgeverijaspekt.nl

Omslagontwerp: Mark Heuveling
Binnenwerk: Thomas Wunderink

ISBN: 9789461535511
NUR: 680

Alle rechten voorbehouden. Niets van deze uitgave mag worden verveelvoudigd, opgeslagen in een geautomatiseerd gegevensbestand of openbaar gemaakt, in enige vorm of op enige wijze, hetzij elektronisch, mechanisch, door fotokopieën, opnamen of enig andere manier, zonder voorafgaande toestemming van de uitgever.

Voorzover het maken van kopieën uit deze uitgave is toegestaan op grond van artikel 16B Auteurswet 1912 j° het Besluit van 20 juni 1974, St.b. 351, zoals gewijzigd bij het Besluit van 23 augustus 1985, St.b. 471 en artikel 17 Auteurswet 1912, dient men de daarvoor wettelijk verschuldigde vergoedingen te voldoen aan de Stichting Reprorecht (postbus 882, 1180 AW, Amstelveen). Voor het overnemen van gedeelte(n) van deze uitgave in bloemlezingen, readers, en andere compilatiewerken (artikel 16 Auteurswet 1912), dient men zich tot de uitgever te wenden.

Table of contents

I.	Early life	13
II.	Cadet school	17
III.	Military service and World War I	22
IV.	Prisoner of war	34
V.	Return to Hungary	38
VI.	Pre-war assignments	46
VII.	Outbreak of World War II	52
VIII.	Hungary's entry in the war	65
IX.	Field command	71
X.	Recalled to Budapest	89
XI.	The final months of the war	99
XII.	Armistice and captivity	111
XIII.	Release and life in Germany	123
XIV.	Emigration to the USA	131
List of sources		139

Foreword

Lieutenant-Field Marshal Jenő halmaji Bor was born on 8 September 1895 and passed from this world on 30 November 1979. During the course of his long life, this Hungarian patriot experienced the history of the 20th Century in the making, having participated as a combatant in both world wars. This book is an account of his interesting life, which, thankfully, the General recounted for posterity, completing his narrative in July, 1971.

I am deeply grateful to General Bor's son, Eugene De Bor, for having taken the time to translate his father's memoirs, and for granting me permission to edit and publish them. I have tried to keep this editing to a minimum, in order to preserve as much as possible the author's original writings. My main contribution to this work is the compilation of the footnotes, which I have used to provide clarification and greater detail about the personalities that General Bor interacted with and referenced in his memoirs.

I would also like to thank my good friend vitéz Zoltán Kőrössy for providing some of the photographs of General Bor.

There is a saying, "Information not shared is lost" and General Bor's contributions to the history of his native land, as a senior military officer, certainly merit sharing. As a proud member of the International Hungarian Military History Preservation Society, I am honored to be a part of this endeavor.

Andris J. Kursietis

Table of ranks

The following table shows the ranks used in this book, and their German and Hungarian denominations.

It should be noted that Major-Generals had one star on their collar rank tabs, Lieutenant-Field Marshals had two stars, while Colonel-Generals had three stars. Until 1941, three-star Generals held the ranks of General of Infantry, Artillery or Cavalry, or Master-General of Ordnance, depending on their branch in the Armed Forces. These ranks were replaced by Colonel-General (vezérezredes) in August of that year.

The rank of Field Marshal in the Hungarian Army could be attained only during war-time. No such rank was awarded during the Second World War. Only Archduke József held the rank of Field Marshal, which he had gained in World War I, and he did not hold an active position in the military after 1918, although he often appeared at official functions in Hungary in his Field Marshal's uniform. (It should be noted that the unique Austrian and Hungarian rank of Lt.Field Marshal is often mistranslated as Field Marshal in English-language documents. The rank is equivalent to a Major-General in the U.S. Army, Generalleutnant in the German Army).

Rank	German	Hungarian
Field Marshal	Generalfeldmarschall	Tábornagy
Colonel-General	Generaloberst	Vezérezredes
General of Artillery	General der Artillerie	Tüzérségi tábornok
General of Cavalry	General der Kavallerie	Lovassági tábornok
General of Infantry	General der Infanterie	Gyalogsági tábornok
Master-General of Ordnance	Feldzeugmeister	Táborszernagy
Lieutenant-Field Marshal	Generalleutnant	Altábornagy
Vice-Admiral	Vizeadmiral	Altengernagy
Captain-General (River Forces)		Vezérfőkapitány
Major-General	Generalmajor	Vezérőrnagy
Rear-Admiral	Konteradmiral	Ellentengernagy

Lieutenant-Field Marshal Jenő halmaji Bor in April 1945

Lieutenant-Field Marshal Bor meeting with German officers

I. Early life

I was born in Hajdúszoboszló (in eastern Hungary) on 8 September, 1895. At that time, my father, János Bor, was the principal of the local Reformed (Calvinist) Church's elementary school - he was later to become director of local public food distribution. My mother, Ilona Rácz, was the daughter of the director of the local land registry office. I was the first of four children in the family; following me was my younger brother László and my two sisters, Ilona and Jolán.

My father was an energetic man with many interests. Aside from being the principal of a large elementary school, he founded the local newspaper and became leader of the local branch of the Independence and '48-ers political party. The name of the newspaper was Független Hajdúság[1] (translated as "Independent Hajdúság"); it was published once a week and, in addition to the local news, carried abbreviated news items from the papers in Budapest. The editorial office was in the Gazdakör building on Rákoczi utca (street). One of the privileges of owning the newspaper was that my father was entitled to a free pass on the national rail lines. Moreover, each summer he received a free family pass for six persons, for a period of two months. When my brother and I were aged 10 and 8 respectively, he took us - along with two or three boys who were the sons of a friend - on a trip across Hungary. We even traveled with him once to Austria, once to Italy, and once to Romania.

One trip was on the lower Danube from Bazias to Vaskapu (Iron Gate) to Ada Kaleh Island. Another trip was to the Adriatic Sea and across to Venice, and yet another was to Székelyföld[2], where

---

1 Hajdúság is a geographic region in eastern Hungary, the people of which were known for their Protestantism and political independence.
2 A part of Transylvania.

we stayed at Málnásfürdő for several weeks before passing through Brassó and crossing into Romania to Sinaia. Our fourth trip took us to Vienna, from there to Salzburg and then the Bavarian border. I was unable to accompany my father on the next trip because I had to prepare for the entrance examination for military school. Other vacations included a summer visit to Bártfa with my mother, and a winter trip to Cirkvenica (on the shores of the Adriatic), from where I returned by myself, even though I was only ten years old.

We also visited relatives in Sarkad. These visits usually took place during the Easter vacation. My father's oldest two brothers, Áron and Lajos, had a lucractive retail business there. Áron was single and great hunter; their sister, my aunt Mari, was also unmarried and kept house for them even though Lajos was married with three children.

Áron was a great story teller. During the Hungarian occupation of Bosnia in 1878, he had served there with a battalion of the Hódmezövásárhely infantry regiment and had attained the rank of squad leader. He could not become an officer because he had not graduated from high school, having to leave school prematurely to earn a living for his family when his father - my grandfather - died young. This is how he became a shopkeeper.

Uncle Áron's stories revolved around Hungarian soldiers serving in Bosnia or Serbia, and were based on real events. They usually involved an assistant surgeon of the battalion who was nicknamed by the soldiers as "assistant doctor William Tell" because of his resemblance to a character on one of the cards in a pinochle deck.

In Sarkad, there was quite a number of people who were related to us, including the notary public of the town and the manager of the Almássy estate, Pál Búzás. When I was already a cadet at military school, Búzás took me to the nearby summer maneuvers on the Alföld (Great Plain) in 1912. There I witnessed an interesting but foolhardy cavalry attack against dug-in and fortified infantry. The general overseeing the maneuvers stopped the attack and ordered the cavalry to return to base. This was my last visit to Sarkad before World War I. Although I as serving in the k.u.k. (Imperial and Royal) artillery regiment in Nagyvárad, I never had the opportunity to visit nearby Sarkad. In the summer of 1914, the Great War started and I was not able to return to Sarkad until the summer of 1920, following the end of the war after which I spent some time as a prisoner of war of the Italians. During this return visit, my uncle Áron recounted the following story.

During 1918, the people elected him to be the town judge. He held on to this office during the Communist regime of Béla Kun[3], and even during the Romanian occupation. During the Communist rule two agents from the county central office arrived by car and stormed into his office to demand that he arrange for the collection of several food items and their delivery to the central office. When he refused, citing the needs of the local sugar mill, a violent argument ensued. As the windows to Uncle Áron's office were open, the whole thing could be heard out on the street. Soon the door flew open and, led by a husky young man from the flour mill, a bunch of men armed with cudgels entered. They screamed at the two agents to leave immediately, or they would be beaten to death. Trembling with fright, the two agents scrambled into their car and sped away. Afterwards the young man with the cudgel (whose name was Seres, and who was related to my uncle) revealed with pride that he had tended my horse while my unit was stationed in Albania. I then remembered that back in 1916 Seres had asked to see me. He wanted to be granted leave ahead of his turn in order to attend his sister's wedding. I had asked my sergeant when Seres' was due for leave and was informed that this was four months away. I therefore refused his request. That evening, after the feeding of the horses, my sergeant reported to me that Seres had spread the oats for my two horses on the ground before them, as a result of which they were unable to feed. I went to the stall and

---

3   Béla Kun (1886 - 1938) was a Hungarian revolutionary who led the Hungarian Soviet Republic in 1919.

saw Seres sitting there watching my horses standing with hanging heads. I yanked Seres to his feet and smacked him twice, ordering him to pick up the oats, put them in proper feedbags, and feed the horses as he had been trained to do. I walked away and forgot about the whole incident. Four months later Seres took his leave as scheduled.

When I heard the story from my uncle about what had happened with Seres and the agents, I immediately sought out Seres and throwing my arms around him thanked him for saving my uncle from those two bandits. His hair covered with flour and with a red face, he protested vehemently. When I mentioned the two smacks that he had received from me, he replied that deserved as much and I should not even mention the incident.

II. Cadet school

My father's income was not sufficient to pay tuition for all his four children, so he tried to obtain scholarships for each of us. Thus in 1909, after I had finished eighth grade, I was accepted as a first-year cadet in the sole artillery cadet school of the Austro-Hungarian Empire. My tuition was paid by the state. The school was located near Vienna, in Traiskirchen. The language of instruction was German, with the exception of three subjects. It was here that I learned German, and finished my training with overall average results. Biology, solid geometry, and tactics were my favorite subjects; in these I excelled, but I did not put much effort in the others. Even later I was always only an average student.

Emperor Franz Josef, at the behest of Hungarian Prime Minister Count István Tisza, ordered the establishment of a separate class for the Hungarian students in the school. Although well-intentioned, this turned out to be a disadvantage to us individually because the students of the other nationalities were envious of us. There were even professors who treated us with enmity. This is how I became acquainted with the cancer of the Monarchy - the hostility among the nationalities. With the exception of the Czechs, we got along fairly well with the other nationalities, but with the Czechs we brawled a lot.

My first year at the school was very tough. It was not so much because of the strict military rules, but because I did not know the language. This caused me a lot of misunderstandings and grief. Around Christmas of the first year I decided that I would leave the school. Then, one evening, when as a result of a mistake of mine my room commander ordered a punishment, I broke out in tears and hold him that I could not stand it any longer. The fellow happened to be a Hungarian-Swabian and took pity on me. He tried to console me: "Don't feel bad now, it's going to get even worse!". However, with his friendly guidance I weathered the crisis; by spring I became accustomed to the new order and my command of the language also improved.

My class had ninety cadets, divided into three sections. The third section contained the Magyars, totalling twenty-six: Swabians from western and southwestern Hungary, Romanians from Transylvania, Slovenes from the northern mountains, and Magyars from the Alföld (Great Plain). Yet we all counted ourselves as Hungarians and stuck together through thick and through thin. As a result of this, we all suffered together for a month, because of the following incident.

The only places where we were permitted to smoke were the canteen and the social hall. Naturally the cadets smoked at other places, such as the latrine, given the chance. Sometimes we even lit up during the study hour when the professor or inspections officer was absent from the classroom. On one such occasion the inspections officer was First Lieutenant Ksoska, who hated Hungarians with a passion and called us "Huns" with derision. He smelled smoke in the classroom during study hour and demanded that those who had been smoking turn themselves in. First one or two stood up, then, as if by command, the whole class. For this Ksoska reported us to our battery commander and we were ordered to fall out in full field uniform every day at 10:00 a.m. for an entire month. Lieutenant Ksoska supervised; anyone who moved while standing to attention he ordered to be confined in the brig.

Another of our battery officers was First Lieutenant Gonzsorovszky, a Pole. He was a gentleman from head to toe, he was wealthy, came from a good family, and he liked us. He limped because of a riding accident. He was friend to us, even to the point that if one of us found himself in some financial difficulty, he would float a small loan, which had to be repaid strictly within the designated time.

Our battery commander was Captain Syrowy, whose home was in the Sudetenland. We hardly ever heard his voice. Three of our professors were Hungarian. First Lieutenant Lenkey, who was a descendant of the famous Captain Lenkey of the 1848 Revolution, taught us physics and chemistry. Dr. Lipter, the regimental surgeon, taught biology and health, and Captain Pumb taught history of Hungarian literature. The course we enjoyed the most was in German literature, taught with great passion by Major Miornyi. When he lectured about Goethe's death and spoke the writer's last words "mehr Licht" - "more light" - tears were streaming down his cheeks. In our fourth year our tactics professor was an artillery staff major; he liked me and I like him.

Among my classmates was Cadet Korell, a Swabian from southern Hungary who finished first in the entire graduating class. As I write these memoirs (1971), he lives here in Baltimore. Rudi Frankovszki was a talented violinist who organized several string quartets. Our best horseman was Cadet Stodolni, who was killed in action in World War I. I had two friends, Baron István Splényi, who after the war entered the industrial field and eventually became chief executive officer of one of Hungary's largest corporations; the other was János Helle, who became a chemical engineer after the war and drifted into extreme right-wing politics.

Each year in the summer we bivouacked at Steinfeld for our field artillery exercises. The location could be reached by a 20-kilometer ride south of Traiskirchen. During the summer of the third year we spent six weeks near Sankt Poelten practicing map making. The fourth summer we rode three days to the south again. Along the way, at the end of each day's march, we were guests in summer resort towns. Dancing until midnight and riding all day made me so exhausted that I slept for 24 hours upon returning to the school. Before commissioning, we spent three weeks at war games in upper Austria, Tyrol and Carinthia.

During the winter of my second year we went skiing on the nearby Anninger mountain. It was very windy and I was badly chilled, and became so seriously ill that I was granted two months of convalescent leave. Nevertheless, I finished the school year.

Our artillery exercises at Steinfeld were quite interesting. We had a chance to use a variety of artillery pieces, including those of 1861 vintage and the most modern ones, except the 30.5 cm mortar which was only demonstrated to us.

From an artistic point of view our orchestra was noteworthy. Several of my classmates played in it and at one point the conductor was also a classmate of mine. One of the Austrian cadets was an excellent piano player, and also composed songs. Orators, minstrels, and other performers abounded and with the orchestra we put on successful artistic evenings. Sometimes we invited magicians from Vienna.

Our dance instructor was the retired dance master from the Vienna Opera House. During the pre-Lenten season we were invited to the balls in nearby Baden. Ten to twenty cadets were sent to these balls with orders to keep any and all ladies dancing and entertained.

On Sundays we went to the theater in Baden. Naturally we made a first stop at the pastry shops. One time Pista Splényi, I and two other Hungarian cadets burst through a revolving door into the pastry shop, bumping into a stout and spunky older gentleman. He exclaimed, "the world is full of shit and bastards are the trump; you fellows Hungarians?". When we nodded, he invited us to be his guests. Naturally we consumed all the cream rolls in the place.

When we went to Vienna (there was a streetcar that took us there), we headed for the Opera House or the Burg Theater where, for twenty Groschen, we got in as standees. Only the military and palace officials were entitled to this privilege. The standing areas were in the back on the ground floor and the view was excellent.

In 1912 the Hunter's Exhibition was held in the Prater in Vienna. Besides all sorts of hunting trophies and game animals there were many other amusements. While it was open we spent all our Sundays there. Once, Emperor Franz Josef and Leopold, King of the

Belgians, drove out there and we had to form the cordon. This was the only time in my life that I saw two kings, or an emperor and a king to be more precise, together in person.

At the end of each school year we had a sports festival, where all of us had to participate. I floor-vaulted with several others. Each festival was attended by Archduke Leopold Salvator[4], the Inspector-General of Artillery.

On 18 August 1913 I was commissioned as Second Lieutenant at a splendid ceremony and left for leave until the end of September on that same day. On 1 October I reported for duty to the commander of the 34th Imperial and Royal Artillery Regiment, in Nagyvárad[5].

---

4   Generaloberst Archduke Leopold Salvator, Duke of Tuscany (1863 - 1931).
5   Now Oradea, in Romania.

III. Military service and World War I

On the basis of the major nationalities represented, the 34th Imperial and Royal Artillery Regiment was bilingual, Hungarian and Romanian. The command language was German. The officers conversed in German, and virtually each nationality of the monarchy was represented among them. We were still at peace, and consequently my military duties consisted of peacetime training routines.

Nagyvárad provided an opportunity for a lively social life. It was derisively nicknamed the "Paris on the Körös" after the river that flowed through the town. We participated in many delightful activities. Aside from the pre-Lenten series of glamorous balls, we usually spent the weekends at our reserved tables in our coffee house, reading, playing chess, billiards and so forth.

One of our comrades, First Lieutenant Béla Losonczi, was a volunteer for aviation training and was always ready to be a daredevil. One late night on our way home, he started to cross the Körös river bridge by walking on one of the supporting arches. It was wide enough to walk on and high enough so that the power lines for the streetcar were suspended from the cross beams. It was winter and early in the morning, and the arches were slippery with ice. Béla managed to reach the highest point, but then dared not proceed any further. He crawled out to one of the cross beams and sat on it with feet dangling, waiting. Because of the height he did not dare to jump. Presently a solitary Gypsy, with a bass fiddle on his back, started to cross the bridge. As he came close, Béla yelled down, "Gypsy, throw down your bass!". The Gypsy screamed, threw down his fiddle and ran back off the bridge yelling until a policeman grabbed him. To the policeman he sobbed, "The Devil took my fiddle!". The policeman, with the Gypsy following at some distance, returned to the bridge to investigate. After he had established that there was no devil around, only a very cold First Lieutenant on top of the bridge, he summoned the fire brigade who, with a ladder, removed the Lieutenant. The whole town laughed about the incident, but the regimental commander confined Béla to quarters for a few weeks. Poor Béla gave his life as an aviator in the World War that followed.

On 28 July 1914, my regiment was ordered to war. Until November 1915, I fought against the Serbians. I took part in the offensive directed by Potiorek[6]; I was on the northernmost wing. We almost reached Semendria when, because of the defeat of our forces on the southern wing, we were ordered to withdraw. During the offensive part of the campaign, it was the artillery that won battles on several occasions.

In 1915 I took part in the Mackensen[7] offensive in which we advanced through Belgrade as far as Kragujevac, but were then withdrawn from there to Arad to be rearmed. We received brand-new mountain artillery pieces, and were then ordered to take part in the conquest of Montenegro and Albania.

In the campaign against Montenegro we participated only as reserves with our newly-organized mountain artillery battery. Artillery support was provided by 24 cm and 30.5 cm mortars and naval units offshore. On the 2,800 meter (9,200 feet) high Mount Lovčen, the mortar rounds did not explode. We found many unexploded shells as we reached the plateau, where we were hit by a snow storm and forced to make camp. I found that our horses formed circles, with their heads together and rumps turned to the wind. Our tents, packed with snow on the outside, could be adequately heated up with a single candle within five minutes.

---

6   Feldzeugmeister Oskar Potiorek (1853 - 1933), Governor-General of Bosnia-Herzogovina in 1914 when the Austrian heir to the throne, Archduke Franz Ferdinand, was assassinated in Sarajevo, precipitating World War I.

7   German Generalfeldmarschall August von Mackensen (1849 - 1945), commander-in-chief of Army Group Mackensen, comprising of both German and Austro-Hungarian units.

King Nicholas of Montenegro[8] fled by aeroplane. His palace, a building that looked like a country mansion, could be visited in Cetinje. In the center hall were huge oil portraits of the Tsar and Tsarina of Russia, and on a table in the reception room was a gift from Franz Josef, a statuette "The Good Shepherd", made of gold.

The town of Cetinje was small. The headquarters of the 20th Mountain Artillery Group, of which we were a part, was set up there and the troops bivouacked in the surrounding country. During our stay there, one late night the commander of the Group communications company was returning from leave. The quartermaster assigned him quarters, but for some reason he chose to sleep in another house. Exhausted, he dropped onto a couch in a room to sleep. What happened during the night was never told by the Lieutenant, but the next morning he was ordered by the commander of the Group, Colonel Vincze nagyjókai Farkas, to report to him. He berated the Lieutenant severely for causing the commander to be involved in an international incident. "Do you know who the woman was that you molested?" asked the Colonel. "I haven't the vaguest idea, my Colonel", replied the Lieutenant. "King Nikola's sister-in-law, you idiot!" came the reply, along with one week of confinement to quarters.

Not long afterward we were ordered to march to Scutari (Shkoder) in Albania, passing through Bari, a seaport. My soldiers complained bitterly about the strenuous march on the rocky roads. I decided to dismount and march with them. We covered about 30 kilometers from Bari to Scutari and when we arrived my legs cramped and I could barely move around. In Scutari we found a few Serbian officers who had become separated from their units.

I achieved a notable feat of arms during the attack on the Italian defense circle around Durazzo when, accompanied by storm troops, my artillery unit broke through the defenses. For this I was awarded the Military Cross, Third Class. Following this, the com-

---

8   Nikola I, King of Montenegro (1841 - 1921) reigned from 1910 - 1918.

mander of the 20th Mountain Artillery Group, Colonel Farkas, ordered me to reconnoiter the Italian fortifications at Valona, with a unit specially equipped for this purpose. Facing these fortifications from our side were scattered outposts manned by Albanian mercenaries under the command of our officers.

On one occasion the mercenaries of one such unit failed to receive either food or pay for one week, and therefore pulled back from their positions and congregated at their main command post in a monastery. They sent word that until they received food and pay, they would not serve. Spring floods were the reason for the delayed supplies, as they had ripped away the draw ferry on the Semeni River. A replacement was not yet ready, and bridges across the river were non-existent.

The Albanian troops were nominally under the command of Achmed Bey[9], whose staff consisted of three Austro-Hungarian artillery officers. One of these was First Lieutenant Tomljenovics, who went out to quiet the mutinous troops. He spoke Albanian because before the war he had served in the mixed-European army of Prince Wied[10] as a battery commander in Durazzo. On his way to the monastery he chanced to meet me and asked me to accompany him, explaining what had happened. Both of us were on horseback and each of us had an orderly who was also mounted. At the monastery, the two orderlies and I stood off to the side as Tomljenovics banged on the huge locked gate with his riding crop. The gates opened slowly and in the yard we could see the whole detachment, with weapons at their feet, standing in a semicircle with their Albanian leader alone in the middle. Tomljenovics rode up to him and knocked him out with one swift blow of his riding crop. Turning to the rest of them, he shouted that the whole

---

9   Ahmet Muhtar Bej Zogolli (1895 - 1961) took the surname Zogu in 1922, and led Albania as President (1925 - 1928) and as King Zog I (1928 - 1939). While serving the Austro-Hungarian Empire, he held the rank of Colonel.
10 Prince William of Wied, Prince of Albania (1876 - 1945) ruled Albania as King Skanderbeg II during six months in 1914 before departing for exile.

regiment was coming up behind him and would put them to the sword if they did not obey his commands. Discipline was restored immediately, and when they heard that floods were the reason for the delay in receiving their supplies they fell on their knees and begged for forgiveness.

How First Lieutenant Tomljenovics became stationed in Durazzo prior to the war, and his activities there, is an interesting footnote to history. At the end of the Balkan War of 1912, the major powers created an independent Albania and established Prince Wied as regent. Wied leaned on the Austro-Hungarian Empire for support while his opposition - Essad Pasha[11] - was Italy's man. The Dual Monarchy kept a cruiser and a mountain artilley unit in Durazzo, along with units of the other powers. Tomljenovics was one of the officers from the artillery unit; he was an adventurous, brave Croatian. He made friends with young Albanians of the Wied party and learned to speak their language. In disguise he took part in several political "excursions".

Essad Pasha had a nice villa on the outskirts of Durazzo, where he lived most of the time. About two or three miles from the villa were the grounds where the troops of the international contingent exercised. Each day a bunch of young Albanian men watched the maneuvers. One day, Tomljenovics was using the grounds with his artillery battery. He called a bunch of young men over to his unit and started to explain to them how the artillery pieces worked, and how they were fired with a draw rope. The next day, when they knew it all, he loaded the two pieces with live ammunition and aimed them at Essad's villa. He handed the draw ropes to a couple of the youths and told them to yank on them once he reached the mess area and gave them a signal. They followed his instructions… the rounds did not hit the villa, but came close enough.

---

11   Essad Pasha Toptani (1863 - 1920) served as Prime Minister of Albania during 1914 - 1916.

Those two shots and the ensuing uproar were heard all the way in Vienna. The Italian government lodged a sharp protest and Tomljenovics was ordered by the monarchy's war minister to be confined on the cruiser for several weeks. He spent his time on the *Empress Elizabeth*, against whose captain he developed eternal hatred because the latter did not permit any easing of the circumstances of his confinement. After he had served out his time, the Lieutenant was ordered back to duty in the monarchy.

At the end of spring, I completed my assignment and returned to my battery, which, along with a second one, was transferred to Kavaja. By that time the number of my troops had drastically declined. With the exception of two volunteers, everybody had contracted malaria. The severe cases ended up in hospitals, or dead.

In the fall I received orders from my commander to lead the two batteries across the Albanian Alps into Macedonia to join the 11th German Army. I reported that the loss of manpower due to the malaria epidemic as so great that the batteries were not fit to move. I was ordered to hire Albanians to make up the deficit. I replied that my march would take four days over little-traveled, unsecure territory (narrow, rocky mountain paths, wild and uninhabited land) and with an untrustworthy crew I could not accept responsibility for reaching my destination safely. I requested soldiers from any nationality of the monarchy to make up the deficit, otherwise I could not accept the assignment. I received a reprimand from my commander for my attitude, but he did send forty infantrymen for each battery from the Lemberg Militia Regiment, with whom I commenced the long trek.

All equipment, including the artillery pieces, had to be packed on small Bosnian pack horses, but at several dangerous passages we lost several horses and their packs. On the fifth day we arrived in Ochrid (at the northern tip of Lake Ochrid) from where I had to send my own battery to Pogradec while the other battery I had to lead to Monastir (Bitoj) where I deployed it behind a Bulgarian corps. I led the fire of the battery under German command until the end of December, when a new battery commander arrived. I eventually returned to my own battery which by then was enplaced against French positions southeast of Pogradec.

When I reached Pogradec I was met by a surprise. I found the 20th Militia Mountain Group there under a new commander, a good-humored colonel from Vienna. Operating in conjunction with the Group was an international community that consisted of Austro-Hungarian diplomats, and German, Bulgarian, Turkish and Greek liaison officers and their assistants. Our former consul from Monastir and his wife were there, along with the former German military attaché to Athens (General Staff Major Bülow). The Greek liaison officer was a First Lieutenant by the name of Miltiades. In addition to Switzerland, this was the only point where the monarchy had contact with the outside world. This was the reason for all these people being there. The Queen of Greece sent her confidential letters to her brother, German Kaiser Wilhelm, through Pogradec. The courier was an adventurous lady, of Hungarian origin and the wife of Prince Ypsilanti, who after a three-day horseback ride through rough terrain and a couple of days rest, continued her journey by motor boat and train to Berlin. The Princess was escorted across the Greek-Albanian border by a solitary footman.

Initially, the Group had three of its battalions deployed in defensive outpost fashion, with big gaps between them. My battery covered the entire deployment from a central position. Across from us were the French, numbering battalion strength, anchored to the southern shore of Lake Ochrid with the other flank open. Near the little town of Korce, which we could observe from our positions, they had a small airfield; from time to time they flew over our positions from there.

On April Fool's Day in 1917, I woke up to a beautiful sunny day. After I surveyed the terrain from my observation post I decided to order an air-raid alert for my battery, which would also apply to the supply train. The latter had to move to a nearby patch of woods in case of such an alert. I sounded the alarm on the field telephone, which action causing the ensuing pandemonium. As soon as I had called off the alert, Group HQ was calling me. The Group artillery commander was asking me whether it was I who had ordered the alert for the Group? I reported that I only ordered the alert for my battery. Beside himself, he yelled that I should have know that by using the field telephone my alert did not remain confined to my battery. He viewed this as spreading false rumors, and was thinking of court-martialling me. Then he slammed the phone down.

Crestfallen, I sat down to think. Ten minutes later I was called again on the telephone. This time it was the Group commander's adjutant. Between long bursts of laughter he told me that he was transmitting the Group commander's message. The Colonel was letting me know that he had not fallen for my prank. "But," he told me, "I whisper in your ear that the whole bunch down here, women and men alike in gowns and britches, ran headlong "to the air-raid shelters and sat there staring at each other…" This is how my April Fool's trick turned out. The next time we had a dinner at Group command, they sat me next to Princess Ypsilanti. "So you were that naughty prankster?" she asked me with a twinkle in her eye.

The foregoing incident happened not long after my arrival. When I surveyed the position assigned to my battery, I realized that we were in no position to cover the whole sector as deployed, and therefore split the battery into two sections positioning each behind one of the flanks. Including myself, we had three officers and two officer candidates. Thus, one officer and one candidate were assigned to each section, and the third officer acted as relief every two or three days.

The front was usually quiet except for one incident when our strongpoint near the lake received a very brisk assault from the French. Even the artillery section sustained losses. It turned out later that the Greek liaison officer befriended one of my officers, who took him for a picnic at a forward observation point. From there he went over to the French and described our positions to them. Naturally, they took advantage of this intelligence. Only with a counterattack were we able to dislodge the French. The Greek disappeared, of course, and Group did not request a replacement.

Once a month, the Group commander invited the battalion commanders and battery commanders, along with one of their officers, to dinner. This way I became acquainted with the members of the international community who were also invited on these occasions. Princess Ypsilanti was also a regular guest whenever she stopped over, and always came in the company of Major Bülow.

The ethnic make-up of the population in Albania and Macedonia, and the regions in between, was mixed. The well-to-do were Turkish and Moslem and they were concentrated in the towns. The most ancient stock, the Skipetars, are lean and tall people. These lived in the hills and mountains, and were Eastern Orthodox Christians. The flat river-bank areas were populated by so-called Kucu-Vlahs. With these my artillerymen from Transylvania who spoke Romanian could carry on a conversation if they used simple words. I did not find out which religion these people professed to, but they were on the lowest rung of culture. They were quite small in stature.

The officers were always quartered in the Turkish residences. There the harems were blocked off from the guest quarters. On the Monastir front, however, only a Kucu-Vlah village was available for quartering my battery. The cottages had thatched roofs and were built with mud and rocks. Through the entrance was a small stall where there were usually a goat and hens (and sometimes a pig). To the right, past the stall, was the living room, and to the left another room with an open hearth. They used dung for fueling the fire. While at Monastir, I went back to my quarters to clean up only once; the rest of the time I cleaned up in the open. The owner of the quarters assigned to me was a soot-blackened woman with a 14-year old daughter. When she was told that the "commendari" was coming, she insisted on meeting me. She brought in her daughter - a dirty, unkempt pubescent girl - and respectfully offered her for my use as I pleased. I was surprised, but thanked her quickly and told her that I did not have the time now.

In the Pogradec area my quarters were in the home of a Turkish farmer. It was a two-story building. The ground floor was occupied by stalls and rooms for farm equipment. The entrance to the upper floor was through the cow stalls by means of a flight of wooden steps. On the upper floor, my room was to the right while the harem and kitchen were to the left. I only came back to my quarters once a week to clean up thoroughly. Every time I came and went, there were always two or three women with the cows in the stalls. As soon as they saw me coming they turned away and pulled their skirts from the back over their heads, exposing their behinds toward me. Such were some of my experiences with the local people and customs.

A few weeks after my April Fool's prank, I was ordered home. I had to report to Hajmáskér Artillery School and Training Center, in Hungary, where I was assigned to a training course. While in training there I had a severe recurrence of malaria that I had contracted in Albania. With a 104 degree fever and unconscious, I was transported to Budapest to a hospital. The Hungarian doctors tried various remedies on me for several weeks before they were able to effect a recovery. Then I was sent for several months of recuperative leave, the last of which I spent in Karlsbad, the famous resort in the German Sudetenland.

We had previously suffered bouts of malaria in Albania, but there we had access to a good supply of foreign-made quinine which we scrounged from the pharmacies left behind by the Italians when Durazzo was captured. When we had an attack, we took about half a packet (approximately 4-5 grams) of quinine and even though we could not hear for a couple of days from the noise in our ears, by the fourth day we were all right. Back home there was only synthetic quinine available, which was much weaker. Treatment was more complicated and in the end the doctors sent their patients to Karlsbad.

Karlsbad was a beautifully-built town famous for its baths. It had a huge drinking hall, beautiful hotels and long walking paths in the woods. The town had its own symphony orchestra, which played in the drinking hall during the mornings, in the park coffeeshops in the afternoons, and twice a month it gave a large performance in the Kursalon. Aside from the extensive musical programs there was also a theater, where they mainly played works by Lehar.

Here I made the acquaintance of a girl from Vienna. We visited the musical programs and took long walks in the woods. She was 18 years old and I was 22, and our friendship lasted even after Karlsbad until the end of the war. Her father owned a restaurant on Prater Strasse in Vienna.

After six months of mainly convalescent leave I was ordered to the front again. I was assigned to the 118th Artillery Regiment from Eperjes, becoming the regimental adjutant. By the end of 1917, we were deployed on the front in Bukovina. By then the war against Russia was almost over, and fraternization between the two sides was extensive. Soon we were withdrawn and the regiment was sent to Hadikfalva in Transylvania. The area was populated by Csángo-Székelys, a people of ancient Hungarian stock. In the spring the whole village suffered an epidemic of eye infections. Even the most beautiful girls could barely blink their eyes. Otherwise the village was very neat and clean.

In May 1918 the whole regiment was transported to the Italian front. Here we saw combat on Assiago Plateau, with mountains in the 8,500 feet range. The regimental command was located on the Monte Meletta peak and the batteries were positioned south from there facing the Col del Rosso. We were preparing for the last great offensive. Because the artillery was to be used in a surprise manner we were not allowed to get our bearings using bracketing shots. This took a great deal of theoretical preparation. The batteries had to be retrained for this new procedure as well as for shooting at these high altitudes. The new procedure was invented by the Germans. An artillery major trained me first, a few weeks before the entire regiment arrived, and I then instructed the batteries after they had arrived.

The offensive started on June 15. The day before, the high command made changes to the plans, some of which were not communicated to all the units. We started with bad premonitions. In our sector, the Tyrolean "Edelweiss" Division carried the brunt of the offensive, but after several days of effort it was unable to advance, whereupon the offensive was halted. During the fighting I was slightly wounded in my hand.

For the rest of the war we were fighting from fixed positions. After the November armistice, our retreat route led through the valley of the Brenta River through the town of Trient (Trento) to the road leading to the Brenner Pass. However, by the time that we reached Trient the town was in the hands of Italian and American troops. They detained most of our army, including my regiment.

IV. Prisoner of war

Being a prisoner of war in Italy was an interesting segment of my life. First the officers were taken to Bellagio, a summer resort on the shores of Lake Como. From there we were sent to San Giovanni di Medua, an alpine resort town. Finally, at the end of December, we were transported to the island of Elba. Here we lived in a two-story villa on the seashore.

Our trip to Elba started from the port of Livorno. We were transported on a coal barge, which had fine coal powder on the bottom where we settled. We had a tenor among us who started to sing. As we reached the open sea the waves became quite substantial and the barge began to pitch and roll. Initially there was no trouble, and we enjoyed the singing, but suddenly the singing stopped and tenor became ill. This was the signal for the rest of us, and within minutes all hundred were very sick. This was my first experience of sea-sickness. When we reached Portoferraio and calm seas, we were all well again as if nothing had happened.

In front of the villa the beach sloped gradually into deep water. It was very pleasant for swimming and sunning when the weather was good. We were forbidden from swimming beyond 100 meters, and a wooden dock stretched that far out. The width of our compound was defined by two fences and there were guards posted at the corners. At the end of January (1919) there were a few who dared the water. In February, however, we had storms for several weeks when the sea rolled and thundered night and day, with the waves battering against the stone walls. The howling of the wind made us all deaf, and everyone became ill.

By March the weather improved significantly and we all rushed to swim. When we were not in the water in the evening, we sat on the stone wall admiring the unbelievably-colored low-flying clouds and mist, goldened by the setting sun across the bay. The views were splendid enough to inspire a lyric poet.

Across the bay was Portoferraio. On a promontory jutting into the sea stood exiled former French emperor Napoleon's little castle. The island had iron ore mines and on the southern edge of the town was a large iron furnace and commercial docks.

The bulk of the prisoners were young men. First we just loafed around, but we soon tired of that. We had the opera singer among us (from the Dresden Opera), and each morning he would stand at the end of the dock and sing one Wagner aria after another. There was also an amateur composer among us. I occupied myself with writing poems. This is how our chorus came into being. Among other things, we learned an entire mass so that we could sing each Sunday in a nearby church. The opera singer sang the Ave Maria, either from Gounod or Schubert. Usually only the old women from the town went to the church, but when we sang the church was packed and a crowd stood outside. The priest's eyes filled with tears of joy. In mid-summer we were sent a new camp commandant, one who had previously been a prisoner in a German camp. He forbade us from going to the outside church and surrounded the camp with a double barbed-wire barricade. From then on we sang mass in the back yard of the villa and the locals listened outside the barbed wire.

We also organized literary matinees, learned two short operettas, and gave performances. The Italian officers came to see one, and even though they could not understand the words, they enjoyed the songs.

In addition, we had courses in language, culture, and sciences. One political course, well-intentioned, was on socialism. At that time Communism raged in Hungary. One officer candidate kept talking about this all the time. Once he was lecturing some other youngsters in the canteen about free love. At the end of the table sat, listening, an artillery First Lieutenant from the reserves (in civilian life he was a judge in Graz, Austria). When the young man said, "you can only be sure of the mother, never of the father, the father could be anyone…", the Lieutenant asked him "is this how you think about your own mother?". The young man hesitated but then said "one can never know for certain…". With this the Lieutenant gave the young man two hard slaps on the face, saying "these I give you in your mother's name!", whereupon the session dispersed.

At one time a stray dog showed up in the camp. Everyone petted it and fed it from his own rations. By the end of a month the dog had rounded out and had healthy, shiny fur. Toward the end of the second month it disappeared; nobody knew what had happened to him. Then one day the dog's skin appeared, stretched out to dry on the guards' side of the fence. Our guards had eaten our dog.

Another time our canteen chief was coming by sailboat across the bay with our week's supply of food. Our two cooks were waiting for him on the shore. The chief dropped his sail and used his speed to beach the boat. He was towing a large tuna fish and as he sprang off the boat the chief started to haul the tuna up onto the beach. As the chief gave a final yank, beaching the tuna, a huge fish followed it out of the water with a wave, onto the sand. The shark tried to flop its way back into water, but with no success. The chief screamed in terror, while the shark kept on thrashing. Finally the two cooks beat the shark to death with the two oars from the boat. The canteen chief then gutted the shark, and yelling "pescecane" (Italian for "shark") tied the rope on the shark's tail and headed into the wind with his boat, back to town. He only got a couple of hundred yards when the shark revived and started to pull the boat in the opposite direction. By now all of us were watching and laughing from the shoreline. Finally the chief stuck his oars out and started to row with great vigor. It was only this way that he was able to get the shark to town for sale. Italian law provided a 50-Lire bounty for sharks, and its meat was bought in the market.

One sunny summer afternoon a little boat approached from town. Our lookouts reported that two Italian officers and a woman sat in the boat. When the boat reached the dock and tied up, one of the officers shouted to us, "Capitano Lenhardt!". Next to me Captain Lenhardt exclaimed, "Dear Jesus, they have come for me!". He ran down to the dock and discovered that the woman was a Red Cross lady who was his fiancee, and who had come to visit him. The guards let them use the guardhouse for privacy for a few hours while we mused what a faithful lover was able to do despite a world turned upside down!

Those who had nothing better to do engaged in biological research. One watched an ant colony as it moved from the villa's yard to the second floor of the villa, surmounting all kinds of obstacles in its path. Others studied the mating of beetles that were present in large numbers. There were those who spent their time training lizards. They took lizards into their rooms and fed them flies and other insects until they became accustomed to captivity; then they learned to come out from their hiding place at a given signal, such as scratching the table, to be fed. I myself watched a lizard for hours outside on a sunny rock. It sat there basking in the sun with its mouth open. Suddenly a fly swooped down directly into its mouth. The lizard swallowed once and continued sunning without even a twitch of its tail. To this day I do not know how he did it.

V.   Return to Hungary

Finally we were told that whoever wanted to go to Austria should report to the camp command. I reported, and was sent to an assembling camp for a few weeks. Then in October, we were transported to Vienna, where a Hungarian welcoming commission awaited us. From them we found out that the Communist regime in Hungary had ended, but that part of the county across the Tisza River was still occupied by the Romanians. We were allowed to visit the city only in groups, and had to wear boutonnieres with our national colors - red, white, and green - instead of our officers' stars. The good Viennese were still tearing off such stars from the collars...

The third day we entered Hungary by train. In a camp at Csot we were assembled, documented and checked out politically. From here, after a few other stops, I received an assignment to the military command of Veszprém County. In February 1920, I was ordered to Budapest to join the headquarters unit of the newly organized division based in Debrecen. Together with the units of the division, I entered Debrecen in the spring. En route I stopped at Hajdúszoboszló to visit my parents, sisters and brother, whom I found in good health and without any problems. I served in Debrecen until the fall of 1922, as the adjutant to the artilley commander of the 6th Mixed Brigade[12]. My commander was a fellow officer from my Nagyvárad days and it was an enjoyable duty.

---

12   During peacetime, the main unit of the Hungarian Army was the Mixed Brigade, which typically was composed of an Infantry Regiment, an Artillery Battalion and a troop of Cavalry. Each Mixed Brigade was numbered according to the Military District in which it was stationed. With the onset of World War II, the Mixed Brigades were upgraded to Army Corps, with the 1st - 7th Mixed Brigades becoming I - VII Army Corps.

In 1922 I was ordered to report to the Military Academy in Budapest for general staff officer training[13]. I graduated in 1924, with average results, and became a general staff officer. After a short tour of duty in Tolna, I was ordered to Hajmaskér to be the tactics instructor in the Artillery School. Until 1928, during the summer months I was an instructor there; during the rest of the year I served as a general staff officer of the 7th Mixed Brigade based in Miskolc.

Here I met, fell in love with, and married my wife Klára, whose father - Kálmán Révész - was the bishop of the Hungarian Reformed (Calvinist) Church for the west side of the Tisza River district. We were married in 1926, and our only son, Jenő Kálmán Imre Bor, was born on 23 June, 1928.

I should mention that while I was stationed in Debrecen I continued to study English, which I had begun as a POW in Italy. While in Miskolc, I studied Italian. I passed my exams in both languages with good results. After I passed my staff school exams, the Chief of the General Staff authorized funds for two months of foreign travel, and in September 1930 my wife and I went on a tour of Italy. Our itinerary took us through Austria to Genoa, Rome, Naples, Florence and Venice. We spent five days in each city. In Venice, my wife unfortunately caught a cold.

I served in Miskolc under three brigade commanders[14] until 1931. While there I gave several lectures on military history and wrote a number of articles for the Magyar Katonai Közlöny (Hungarian Military Review). I also authored a politico-military study which I submitted to the Chief of the General Staff of the Hungarian Armed Forces[15]. The subject of the study was the search for a suitable foreign

---

13 On 1 September 1922, Jenő Bor was promoted to Captain, an event not mentioned in his memoirs.
14 General of Infantry Kálmán Révy (1925 - 1928), Lt.Field Marshal Albin Lenz (1928 - 1930), and Lt.Field Marshal Hermann Pokorny (1930 - 1931).
15 General of Infantry Kocsárd Janky (1868 - 1953), who concomitantly held the position of Commander-in-Chief of the Armed Forces during 1925 - 1930.

alliance through the evaluation of the potential of military-industrial production. The outcome of the study was that, objectively, the Soviet Union would have been the best choice for an ally. This was ideologically, and therefore politically, impossible. My study resulted, however, in my being transferred to Budapest from the fall of 1931. After I completed the preliminary and main examinations for staff officer, I was assigned to the Ministry of Defense, Military-Industrial Division (HM 1/c). My transfer to Budapest was unexpected and disrupted my recently-begun family life. We were not prepared for the sudden move. With a few months delay my family was able to follow me and we found an apartment on Márvány utca in Buda.

About the time of my assignment to my new job, the mutual disarmament conference was taking place in Geneva. Most of the participants were re-arming themselves at the same time. My predecessor attended the conference as a technical advisor.

In 1932 I was promoted to Major in the general staff[16]. At the same time I was assigned to the staff of Gergely Tóry, Under-Secretary of State for Commerce, who headed the Industrial Division; I was to study the Hungarian industry. With this assignment my future for the next four-and-a half years was determined. It also influenced my future career.

In the Ministry I studied each industrial sector under the tutelage of the responsible division chief. I discussed my notes and observations with Under-Secretary Tóry and on the basis of these I prepared two studies for the Chief of the General Staff. One study discussed the position of Hungary and the surrounding small nations in the event of a trade blockade. The other study discussed the steps to be taken by Hungary in the case of industrial mobilization for war. Along with the Industrial Division, my other colleagues were Károly Kádas, who later became Under-Secretary of State in the Ministry of Industry, and István Schlick, who was Division Chief for Foreign Trade.

---

16 The actual date was 1 May, 1932.

In order to understand my "blockade" study, it is necessary to know the following background. The charter of the League of Nations authorized the use of commercial blockade as an instrument of sanctions against non-complying nations. Considering the possibility that Hungary and the surrounding countries might become non-complying nations, it was necessary to examine the ramifications. I prepared my study on the basis of all the then-available foreign trade statistics and other sources of information. The objective was to demonstrate the military-industrial weaknesses of Hungary, the countries of the Little Entente[17], and of Austria as well.

We concluded that Hungary could supply its industries and population with fuel, but not with electricity. Heavy industry - the production of iron and steel - stood or fell with the importation of coke and higher-grade iron ore. Oil production was then only in an exploratory stage, although quite promising. In other metals industries only aluminum commanded an ample domestic supply of raw material. Neither copper nor other ores for metals and for alloys were present in the country. The textile industry depended on imports of cotton and flax. For the leather industry we had to import tanning chemicals. The chemical industry was in its infancy; aside from sulphuric acid and saltpeter, there was no other production. Production of pharmaceuticals was fairly well developed. The lumber industry suffered from a gross lack of quality forestry products. Hungary's manufactured goods industry, although possessing adequate technical knowledge and willingness, operated generally with out-dated methods. Its machinery stock was not suited for mass production. For the armed forces, there existed a single gunpowder and explosives factory, one artillery and rifle production facility, and adjunct plants for the manufacture of ammunition in small quantities. Even these plants were antiquated. The food raw material and processing

---

17   An alliance formed in 1920 and 1921 by Czechoslovakia, Romania and Yugoslavia with the purpose of common defense against Hungary and the prevention of a Habsburg restoration. It was disbanded in 1938.

industry was ample, exporting substantial quantities to Central Europe and the West.

As regards Yugoslavia, we established that it did not have coal, oil, or any other significant sources of energy. It had abundant supplies or iron, copper and lead ore but did not have facilities to convert these to metal. The textile industry was minimal in size, but raw materials - mainly wool - were adequate. Also adequate were the leather and lumber industries. Yugoslavia's chemical industry was about equal to that of Hungary, with sodium also being produced. It was remarkable how passive the country was with regard to food production. If the Bácska[18] was taken away, the situation would be catastrophic. In some items, such as wood and small barnyard animals, there was a great abundance, but a critical shortage existed in grains. The finished good industries were in their infancy, and no significant factories or trained personnel existed.

Romania was obviously richly endowed with oil, of which considerable quantities were exported. However, other energy sources were slim. The iron and metals industry barely covered internal needs. All of it was located in Transylvania[19] and owned by Hungarians. Its chemical industry was fairly advanced based on the natural gas wells also located in Transylvania and built with the help of the Germans. The leather industry was developed, but the textile industry barely covered internal needs even though raw materials, with the exception of cotton, were adequate. The finished goods industry was underdeveloped and outdated, and a significant part of it was again located in Transylvania. The food, pasture, and forest production sectors were excellent.

Austria was depicted as an economically unbalanced state. It did not have coal, and oil production was in a developmental stage. The energy sources were mainly based on water power, which in the winter was hardly useable. Otherwise, it had a surplus of pow-

---

18 Northeast Yugoslavia, previously part of Hungary.
19 Transylvania was part of Hungary prior to World War I.

er. Austria's iron and lead ores were adequate but other metals were lacking. The leather industry was similarly limited, although tanning chemicals were available. The lumber industry was excellent, both from the point of view of raw materials and manufacturing. The finished goods industry was tuned to the consumption pattern of the old Austro-Hungarian Empire and was not condemned to idleness in large part. The technicians and skilled workers were emigrating abroad, mainly in the direction of Hungary. Austria's greatest weakness was a lack of foodstuffs. It was in need of sizeable imports for which it had nothing to pay with.

Thanks to the generosity of the Western Powers, Czechoslovakia was given such boundaries after the war that its economic balance was largely assured. With the exception of oil and cotton, it lacked virtually nothing. The country's weakness, we found, lay in its ethnic make-up and military geography.

In summary, the results of the studies forced the following spontaneous conclusions:

1. Hungary, especially, but also the other countries on their own could not possibly resist an economic blockade or conduct war for any length of time. All hostile politics among these small nations should be viewed as tilting at windmills.

2. Economic and political cooperation among these countries of the Danubian Basin was the only solution for a positive situation. The economic, political, and military advantages of a Danubian bloc were attested to by the 400-year success of the Habsburg Monarchy.

My second study concerned itself with the questions surrounding the economic mobilization of Hungary in case of war. It would be too lengthy to recite the many proposals the study put forth. Essentially, basic guidelines needed to be worked out for the following areas, and the responsibility for the execution of these needed to be given to some type of organization.

First of all, prototypes of military equipment needed to be developed by experts. Mass production of these articles - with possible changes - was to be discussed with suitable manufacturing firms. The machinery park of these producers needed to be rearranged or supplemented. To make production easier, simplification of the procedures needed to be achieved.

The prices of the products needed to be pre-determined. Re-equipping of the armed forces was a national endeavor, so profiteering had to be eliminated. On the other hand, the production potential of the industries needed to be sustained or even expanded, so a certain allowance would have to be made for a reasonable level of profit. The industries might even need to be assisted in the acquisition of the required equipment. Price control and monitoring was an economic-political task that needed to be handled by experts.

The available skilled work force was excellent, but small. It needed to be increased tenfold using the old cadre in a training program for new workers. Similarly, the engineering and technical manpower pool needed to be enlarged.

The acquisition of raw materials needed for production and the management of their utilization were the most substantial problems. For this, an Office of Materiel, with powers granted by legislation, needed to be established. Because the country was so poor in resources, stockpiling on a large scale would be necessary. The producers would be responsible for normal production stockpiling, but for six months beyond that the state would be responsible. Stockpiling involved the use of foreign currency, which made it a matter of state and National Bank policy. The production of material from domestic resources also needed to be developed, for which an internal credit policy needed to be established.

A credit policy framework needed to be set up for all of the foregoing. Since this involved both national and international policy matters, it came under the decision-making powers of the Hungarian Parliament.

The study made it obvious that all of the ministries needed to participate in the planning of mobilization. The Ministry of Defense, therefore, proposed to the Cabinet that each ministry establish an organizational unit to deal with mobilization matters. To direct these, a division in the Ministry of Defense was created. The military officers assigned to this unit were the chiefs of the mobilization units in the other ministries. During the organizational phase, I was in charge of the entire process. When it was completed, a general staff Colonel was put in charge, and I was reassigned to be Deputy Chief of Staff of the 1st Mixed Brigade, based in Budapest, in the spring of 1936[20].

The new Division of Mobilization, drawing on the expertise of legal staff, drafted the so-called National Defense Act which it submitted to the Parliament. Parliament adopted the legislation, designating it as "1939.II.t.c.".

Meanwhile, major changes occurred both in Hungary and abroad. In Germany, Hitler had come to power and was banging loudly on the doors of history. The world was fermenting anew. In Hungary, Prime Minister Gyula Gömbös[21] tried to lead the country out of the economic crisis that it, like most Western European nations, had been suffering from since several years. Emphasizing peaceful revision, he wished to build strong ties with the Berlin-Rome Axis.

---

20   On 1 November 1935, Jenő Bor was promoted to the rank of Lieutenant-Colonel.
21   General of Infantry Gyula jáfkai Gömbös (1886 - 1936) served as Minister of Defense during 1929 - 1936, and concomitantly Prime Minister during 1921 - 1936. He died of cancer while still in office.

VI. Pre-war assignments

From 1936 until October 1937 I served initially as Deputy Chief of Staff of the 1st (Budapest) Mixed Brigade and the last six months as acting Chief of Staff. The Brigade commanders were Lt. Field Marshal vitéz[22] Jenő Rátz[23], until the end of the 1936 summer maneuvers, followed by Lt. Field Marshal vitéz Vilmos nagybaczoni Nagy[24]. My service was particularly enjoyable under the latter, when I was temporarily Chief of Staff. The summer maneuvers of 1937 involved the whole Mixed Brigade; they started with a crossing of the Danube and ended with the use of Mobile Brigades at Tiszafüred. With minor exceptions, the entire Hungarian Army participated in the maneuvers.

While I was serving in Budapest, we celebrated the visits of two heads of state, with military parades. The first guest was the President of Austria[25], followed by the King of Italy[26]. In both instances the parade took place on Andrássy út (avenue), moving from Népliget (People's Park) toward the center of the city. All traffic was stopped and each participating unit had to have detailed instructions as to assembly points and march route. Although both

---

22 Vitéz was a title awarded to recipients of the Knightly Order of Vitéz, established to honor heroic deeds.
23 General of Infantry vitéz Jenő nagylaki Rátz (1882 - 1952) commanded the 1st Mixed Brigade during May - September 1936. Rátz went on to be Chief of the General Staff (1936 - 1938), Minister of Defense (1938), and in 1944 served as Deputy Prime Minister of Hungary.
24 Colonel-General vitéz Vilmos lófö nagybaczoni Nagy (1884 - 1976) led the 1st Mixed Brigade during October 1936 - October 1939. He subsequently served as Inspector of Infantry (1939 - 1940), and Commander-in-Chief of the 1st Army (1940 - 1941) before retiring in May 1941. He was recalled in September 1942 as Minister of Defense, until June 1943.
25 Wilhelm Miklas (1872 - 1956) served as President of Austria between 1928 - 1938, until the country's Anschluss with Germany.
26 Vittorio Emanuele III ruled as King of Italy during both World Wars, from 1900 until his abdication in 1946.

the Austrians and Italians awarded many decorations during the visits, we who worked extremely hard on the planning and execution received nothing.

In October 1937 I was called to the office of the Deputy Minister of Defense, Károly Bartha[27]. He asked whether I would accept the position of organizer and head of the Industrial Mobilization Division at the Ministry of Industry.

The Ministry of Industry had been created[28] by Prime Minister Gömbös on the principle that war industry needed a separate ministry in order to be properly organized. The new ministry had come in large part from the old Industry Division of the Ministry of Commerce. A minister[29] and a Secretary of State for Industry were appointed; the latter, Antal Petneházy, was a former classmate of mine and a Lieutenant Colonel in the Corps of Engineers. According to my information, Undersecretary Gergely Tóry was scheduled to retire shortly. Gömbös, in order to assure the effectiveness of his policies, had appointed officers from the Corps of Engineers to certain key positions in the Ministry. Both the Chief of the General Staff and the career civil service corps were strongly opposed to this policy.

After briefly contemplating the situation, I replied to Deputy Minister Bartha that I would accept the position under certain conditions. These were: that Undersecretary Tóry remain in his position; that I get a free hand - with my own budgeting power - to organize the division; and that in order to maintain close relations between the ministries I should be designated Deputy Chief of the Main Materiel Group in the Ministry of Defense. General

---

27   Colonel-General vitéz Károly dálnokfalvi Bartha (1884 - 1964). The author mistakenly names Bartha as the Minister of Defense, but Bartha did not become Minister of Defense until November 1938; in October 1937 he was serving as head of the Ministry's Military Bureau and Deputy Minister of Defense.
28   The new Ministry of Industry was created in August 1935.
29   The first Minister of Industry was Géza Bornemisza (1895 - 1983).

Bartha promised that he would make the necessary proposals and that I should await my appointment.

Shortly thereafter this indeed happened, and I entered the Ministry of Industry. I paid my respects to Minister Bornemisza, and visited the various Secretaries of State (Industry) and division chiefs and, first and foremost, started the organization of my division. From the Ministry of Defense I was assigned two General Staff officers, four officers from the Corps of Engineers, an infantry engineer, and a few other military personnel who were technical experts. From the Ministry of Industy I was given a few career civil servants who were also technical experts. My division was designated Division 17 in the Ministry of Industry, and I was made Deputy Chief of the Main Materiel Group in the Ministry of Defense. My division was divided into three groups: Planning, Manufacturing, and Raw Materials. Later we hired about ten engineers freshly graduated from universities.

Gyula Gömbös had died in October 1936, and Kálmán Darányi[30] replaced him as Prime Minister. Darányi continued the substantial program of equipping the armed forces and announced it publically under the so-called "Györ Program". The Parliament in turn passed the Defense Legislation.

In one move, the 1 billion pengö program[31] to equip the armed forces made the problems of industrial mobilization much easier. The various materiel divisions of the Ministry of Defense issued the procurement orders and established the rules for delivery; we designated the respective producers, and oversaw production scheduling, manpower problems, and timely delivery. Until 1 September 1939, the start of the war in Europe, the whole system worked on the principle of private enterprise. But, with the start of the war, disturbances (speculation) were expected in both the in-

---

30   Kálmán Darányi (1886 - 1939) served as Prime Minister between October 1936 - May 1938.
31   Approximately $200 million.

ternational and domestic markets, therefore, principally to assure raw materials, economic mobilization had to be ordered.

Despite the fact that neutrality would have been the only sane course of action for the country, Hungary gradually became involved in the Second World War. Our rearming was acquiesced to even by the countries of the Little Entente, in an agreement reached at Bled. It was Hitler that they were afraid of...

The first obstacle, or to be more precise the slowing-down factor, to rearmament turned out to be financial. Once the bids were received from industry it was obvious that the 1 billion pengös allocated was not enough: the first step alone required 1.6 billion pengös. Because of this problem, Minister of Economics Béla Imrédy[32] called a conference at the Ministry of Defense. The conference decided that upon delivery of the goods, only 80% of the price would be paid (less, in the case of advance payment) and 20% would be withheld pending a decision by the Price Examining Authority.

Mobilization progressed on the basis of the studies previously mentioned. The greatest problem to be faced was the securing of raw materials. I will return to the details of this issue later.

Germany had been arming at a breakneck speed since 1932, and we were given the unsought opportunity to get an inside view of the process. In 1938, in response to an invitation, I traveled to Berlin accompanied by a General Staff Lieutenant Colonel and a civilian engineer (the raw materials group chief). I did not gain much new technical knowledge as a result of the trip - largely I was operating on the basis of the same principles as they were. However, for self-evaluation purposes the trip was valuable.

---

32   Vitéz Béla ómoravicza Imrédy (1891 - 1946) served as Minister of Economics in the Darányi Cabinet, and replaced Darányi as Prime Minister in May 1938. After the war, he was executed by firing squad in Budapest.

The surprise was that war production was not under a single director. The three branches of the armed forces (Army, Air Force, and Navy) dealt separately with industry. In such a large industrial nation as Germany, they did not feel the need to unify the management of armaments in the hands of one person. Jealousy among the services also played a part in this situation. Only in the headquarters of the High Command[33] was there an overseeing office (under the direction of General Thomas[34]) but it concerned itself only with economic policy and not with the coordination of armaments.

The military personnel that I dealt with were very polite and open with me. They complained only about our military attaché, that he strongly favored the Jews. General Thomas treated me like a member of an allied force. He gave a memorandum that he had written to read, but I was to keep the contents secret. The memorandum gave concrete proposals for the making of military alliances. It proposed that an alliance should be made with either England or the Soviet Union. Either alliance was aimed at gaining a free hand in southeastern Europe (including Hungary). It advised against collaborating with Italy because of her military, and especially economic, weaknesses. Hitler had seen the document.

General Thomas hosted a dinner in my honor in the Adlon Hotel. During this occasion, our military attaché, General Staff Lieutenant Colonel Kálmán Hardy[35], monopolized General Thomas, sitting with him separately while we were having after-dinner coffee. The younger officers drew me to another table and surrounded me. All of their questions were directed at Hungary's opinion of

---

33   OKW - Oberkommando der Wehrmacht, headed by Generalfeldmarschall Wilhelm Keitel.
34   General der Infanterie Georg Thomas (1890 - 1946) headed the Defense Economy and Armaments Office until 1942.
35   Kálmán Hardy (1892 - 1980) served as military attaché in Berlin between 1936 - 1940. He was later (1944) to become Commander-in-Chief of the Hungarian River Forces with the rank of Captain-General, and was posthumously promoted to Colonel-General in 1992.

the new German empire. At first I answered them in generalities, that we were deeply impressed by Hitler and the new German politics. Eventually they popped the big question: were we going to march with them or not? To this I replied, "It is uncertain whether Hungary can march with Germany, but it is certain that it will never march against it…". History, unfortunately, proved me correct.

VII. Outbreak of World War II

After the agreement in Munich between England, France and Germany concerning the handing over of the Sudetenland by Czechoslovakia to Germany, Hungary's demands with the respect to the Hungarian-populated areas of Slovakia were put on the agenda. After long and fruitless inter-governmental negotiations, the German and Italian governments, on the basis of the conference of a commission of judges in Vienna, arbitrarily decided the new Hungarian-Slovakian boundaries.

The Hungarian army marched into the regained northern territories with much ceremony. I participated - unofficially - in two such ceremonial entries. One was from Esztergom into Párkánynána, and the other from the valley of the Bodva River into Kassa (where my wife had been born and raised). The entry into Párkánynána was led by General Vilmos nagybaczoni Nagy[36], commander of the I. Army Corps based in Budapest. The crowds were wildly enthusiastic as the troops crossed the bridge spanning the Danube and entered the flag-bedecked town. Poems were recited by choruses, and bands played during the ceremonial transfer. The crowds shouted, "Return Pozsony, return Nyitra... return Prague!"[37].

The entry into Kassa was accomplished in several marching columns by the Army Corps based in Miskolc. I joined a battalion group that was approaching from the Bodva Valley, and we entered the city from the west. When we crossed the old border - at Nagyida - a 30-member Gypsy band welcomed the battalion and then marched in front of the column like a military band, three large basses tied to the bellies of the Gypsies, and playing. When we reached Kassa, which had been occupied earlier by the main column, I visited relatives in the city while the unit rested.

---

36 See footnote 24.
37 The first two were cities that had not been awarded to Hungary.

We drove back to Budapest through Rozsnyó. General Béla Miklós[38] had entered the town with a mounted brigade. After the ceremony, a large delegation came to pay its respects, and he was requested to proceed to Igló[39] with his unit, because this town also wanted to return to Hungary.

In the spring of 1939, the time finally came for Hungary to occupy the most eastern part of Czechoslovakia. This happened despite the opposition from Hitler's government. At the same time, Germany occupied the rest of Czechoslovakia and established an independent state in the remaining part of Slovakia.

I made a short a trip there, since I wanted to assess the value of the area to the military economy. The large-scale lumber producing and wood distilling establishments, all in German hands (locals), made a very good impression on me. I observed as large rafts of lashed-together logs were propelled from the lakes of the Upper Tisza down river - with great peril - by skilled young men riding them. I saw beautiful elk herds crossing the roads we traveled with jumps of 30 - 40 feet. Between Ungvár and Munkács I saw Jewish farmers sitting on benches in front of their houses on a holiday, resting.

In 1939, even before the economic mobilization, military production was at a high level. There were two items that our experts were unable to design - tanks and airplanes. We therefore wanted to obtain these from the Germans. On 1 September 1939, the situation changed. The Germans attacked Poland but Hungary remained neutral. It did not wish to abrogate the centuries-old Polish-Hungarian ties of friendship.

---

38 Colonel-General vitéz Béla lófö nemes dálnoki Miklós (1890 - 1948) commanded the 2nd Cavalry Brigade at this time. He was later commander of the I. Mobile Corps, IX. Army Corps, and Adjutant-General to the Regent of Hungary, before taking command of the 1st Army in 1944. During December 1944 - November 1945, Miklós served as Prime Minister of the National Provisional Government that had been set up in opposition to the German occupation of Hungary in October 1944.
39 Igló had not been awarded to Hungary.

Nevertheless, mobilization had to be ordered, to forestall disturbances. The Ministry of Industry, under the leadership of Secretary of State Gergely Tóry, established an Office of Raw Materials. This office took charge of the management of all raw materials of military significance. On the same day, the Gazette of (Government) Regulations published the list of critical raw materials and ordered that stocks of such be reported.

From the Industry Mobilization Division we formed a group, the "War Industry Group", consisting of three divisions, XVII/a, XVII/b, and XVII/c. The task of division XVII/a was to designate the plants producing war materiel as "defense plants" and make the necessary arrangements to place the workers under military discipline and assure their exemption from military service. Division XVII/b was charged with establishing production schedules and quality and other controls. Division XVII/c, in collaboration with the Office of Raw Materials, was tasked with establishing the guiding principles for the use of raw materials and substitutes, and with the management for procuring the six-month stockpile and its allocation. Its very first task was to propose to the government that it secure, through the National Bank, foreign currencies worth 40 million pengös to be used for procurement outside of Hungary.

As the head of the War Industry Group, I simultaneously became a member of the National Mobilization Commission, of the Conference Board of Secretaries of State for Economic Matters, and of the Foreign Trade Commission[40].

With the introduction of industrial mobilization, the Public Food Supply Ministry and the Price Control Commission were established. Assuring adequate food supplies for defense factory personnel was an important social consideration.

---

40 In the meantime, on 1 May 1939, the author had been promoted to the rank of Colonel.

After the 1939 campaign against Poland and the 1940 spring offensive against France were over, the Hungarian government felt itself strong enough to press its demands for the return of Hungarian territories in Romanian Transylvania. The German government was determined to block this. Negotiations between representatives of the Hungarian and Romanian governments, initially held in Turnu Severin, did not produce results. The Hungarian government then ordered its armed forces, in the strength of three armies, to be deployed along the Romanian border, and to prepare for an offensive. The German government could not permit this offensive to take place because of the potential for disruption in the flow of oil from Romania during the war. Germany requested that both countries send representatives to Vienna to work out a peaceful resolution to the situation. This Second Vienna Award determined - again capriciously - the new boundaries between Hungary and Romania. Although both sides were compelled to accept it, neither was satisfied.

On orders from Prime Minister Pál Teleki[41], as part of the march into the newly re-acquired territories, I had to lead industrial scouting missions into Transylvania. We were to determine the overall situation, and also the need for any economic aid. My task was to stimulate, with all the means at my disposal, the continuance of production in the industries, even if there were no actual orders in hand for their products.

I traveled throughout the northern half of Transylvania, beginning at Szatmárnéti (Satu Mare). The Regent[42] marched in with the

---

41   Count Pál Teleki (1879 - 1941) had served as Prime Minister of Hungary during July 1920 - Apri 1921, and in February 1939 once again took up this position. While still in office, he committed suicide on 3 April 1941 in protest at Hungary's agreement to assist Germany in the attack against Yugoslavia.

42   Vice Admiral vitéz Miklós nemes nagybányai Horthy (1868 - 1957) led the Hungarian forces that defeated the Communist regime in Hungary in 1919, and the following year was elected Regent of Hungary by the Parliament. He ruled as Regent until being overthrown by the Germans in October 1944.

troops and then had the units of the 3rd Hungarian Army under the leadership of Lt. Field Marshal Vilmos Nagy parade before him in the town square. I visited the saw mills in the surrounding countryside. In one of these I witnessed a moving scene. When I told the Székely owner that I wanted to help him, tears came to his eyes and he said, "Sir, until now when a government man came to me he always demanded money from me… This is a doubly festive day for me. I thank you for the offered help, but now the border is open and I will need no help!". The situation was similar with other small industries. What was remarkable was the coolness with which the leading officials of the local bank initially greeted me. They probably thought that I had come to collect a ransom. As soon as they found out that I was there to help, their faces lit up.

It took two days for the troops to march through. The locals wondered where Hungary had gotten all these soldiers. The next daybreak I overheard two maids talking, "I polished some Hungarian boots this morning. Boy, was it fun!".

The next day we went to Nagybánya (Baia Mare), but the army did not march through this town. We were the only military representatives to come there, and the townspeople, along with the officials from the mines, wanted to celebrate so they treated us to a festive banquet. Things were in order here - production work was continuing. However, the ladies of the town who had Romanian maids complained that the maids had fled because they thought that the Hungarian soldiers would run them through with their bayonets.

The next day we drove to Dés (Dej). Here we found the headquarters staff of the 3rd Army. There were a lot of military personnel and many visitors from the countryside milling around, celebrating. This is where we heard news of the first atrocity. In one of the townships in the Szilágyság region, an approaching Hungarian battalion was greeted with machine-gun and rifle fire. The battalion surrounded the town and took it by force. The battalion commander had the town leaders (priest, teacher, etc.) rounded up and they were summarily shot. The commander was court-martialled, but I do not remember the outcome. Later the Parliament also debated this incident.

In Dés we found no problems - everybody was happy. From here my group split in two, with one part, under my command, moving towards Kolozsvár (Cluj) and the other part, under the leadership of General Staff Captain István báthi Berkó heading towards Marosvásárhely (Târgu Mureş).

Passing through Apahida, bypassing Szamosujvár (Gherla), I reached Kolozsvár from the west. Everywhere my trip took me through flag-bedecked, clean-swept Magyar towns. The people, dressed in their Sunday-best, lined the streets and stopped us and would not let us continue until they had squeezed our hands and we had kissed their children. They were very unhappy that no troops came marching through their towns. Eventually I reached Kolozsvár and was greeted by a resounding cacophony. Four or five marching bands walked the streets playing marches at full blast. At the Mátyás equestrian statue I got out of my car. I had barely taken two steps before a girl threw her arms around my neck and said, sobbing and kissing me at the same time, "Oh! How wonderful that finally you have arrived! You have no idea how much we suffered even during the last minutes." I replied to her, "Well, we are here, so you can be at ease now."

Past the church in the main square, the reviewing stands stood ready for the troops' arrival. The 2nd Army, under the command of Lt. Field Marshal Gusztáv Jány[43], had not yet arrived, except for a few scouting units, making me among the first Hungarians present. We started to acquaint ourselves with the people in the streets, who treated us with all kinds of fine foods and pastries. Meanwhile, it clouded over and then started to drizzle, but the

---

[43] Colonel-General Vitéz Gusztáv Jány (1883 - 1947) was the commander of the 2nd Hungarian Army between 1940 and 1943. He was executed by the Communists following the war, but posthumously rehabilitated in 1993.

troops still had not arrived. Finally Jány entered the town and took his place to review the troops. It took five hours for the parade to pass and General Jány stood in the pouring rain until the very end.

In Kolozsvár we saw the unusual scene of many stores having been looted; this had been done by the population before the military arrived. They said, in response to our questions, that those stores belonged to Romanians or Jews.

Despite the rain, the loud yelling and singing lasted through the night. There were some drunken bands of citizens that rampaged through some parts of the town until the military command restored order. In the evening we had already decided to drive to Beszterce (Bistrita) the next day. We wanted to find out what the Saxon population there had to say.

Arriving in Beszterce we found the town in festive mood. Most of the people were tipsy. A man stopped us and stuck a piece of paper under my nose and said, "Have you ever seen such a miracle? I got this certificate for nothing. I need it for travel. Before you came, I had to bribe the doorman, then the clerk so that I could get to see the judge, and then bribe him to get the paper. It cost me at least 10,000 to 20,000 lei[44]. And now I got it for nothing!".

We ran into quite a few well-dressed men in the streets who spoke "Hochdeutsch" and would not comment on the situation. On the outskirts we visited an ancient iron foundry. It was very dirty but the owner did not ask for help. The place was very busy. From here we drove to Szászrégen[45]. We did not find a soul on the streets. The windows were shuttered, the gates bolted, with the inhabitants in hiding; it made a very bad impression on us.

---

44 At the exchange rate prevalent in 1940, this equated to $50 - $100.
45 A town with a predominantly Saxon (German) population.

Our trip now took us to the Tölgyes Pass. Along the road were several lumber yards, but none of them were working and yards were full of unsold lumber. In Tölgyes I walked into the office of one of the yards and asked for an explanation. I was told that they had not been able to sell anything; the Romanians would not buy the lumber and there was no rail line toward Hungary. The new border severed the main rail line that ran in a large circle in Transylvania. I admonished the people that they had to work and, if needed, the Hungarian government would give them financial help. They took note and said that they would keep operating. While we were talking inside, a crowd gathered outside. When I stepped out all I could see were women, children, and old men. The husbands and young men were still soldiers in Romania. I told them that the coming winter was going to be hard because there would be hardly any work. One of the women replied, "It does not matter, Sir! The important thing is that you are here now. This way, even hungry, we are willing to accept our fate!".

Next we went to Sepsiszentgyörgy. Along the way we saw houses burning in some of the villages, but the people were lining the road to greet the marching Huszars. One of my officers yelled to the Székelys that they should go put out the fires. "These houses need to burn!" was the reply.

The people in Sepsiszentgyörgy had been enthusiastically celebrating for three days. My hostess' maid declared that she would find herself a strapping soldier and would not even come home for a few days. On the third day the town commandant (a Lieutenant Colonel) issued a proclamation that the celebrations had to stop and work must start. He almost had a revolution on his hands: "Are you going to act like the Romanians did? We are not going to stop! Withdraw your order!". The Lieutenant Colonel did indeed rescind the order.

As matters had gotten on the right track here, we had no more to do. Connecting the land of the Székelys with the mother country would have to be done through German mediation, until a rail line to Hungary could be built. The one link for trucks transporting goods was a third-class road south of Déda.

We made a one-day excursion to Lake Gyilkos, which had been created the previous century when half of a mountain broke away. The landslide blocked the flow of a stream and from this was created a deep lake. The enormous fir trees were still visible under the water. There were beautiful villas around the shore, belonging to rich Romanians from the Regat[46]. I then visited my favorite summer place from my childhood, Málnásfürdö. I found that the place had been very much neglected.

From there we traveled through Szováta to Marosvásárhely. With its warm, salty lake Szováta was the favorite summer vacation place of the Romanian royal family. They had a splendid villa on the shore.

In Marosvásárhely we found that a regular civil government had been established. However, the army was guarding the former Romanian church and some other public buildings so as to prevent our good Székelys from setting fire to them. The headquarters of the 3rd Army was located here, despite the strong protests of the Chief of the General Staff, Henrik Werth[47], to the army commander, General Vilmos Nagy. Nagy was very happy that he could once again be where the schools of his youth were located. The town had some natural gas wells, which provided the heating source for the town. I also had a gas stove in my room.

I now ordered the two sections of my scouting party back to Kolozsvár for the purpose of preparing a report on our experiences. While I was working on this, I had an attack of kidney stones and

---

46 The Regat as a part of Romania on the eastern side of the Carpathian Mountains.
47 Colonel-General Henrik Werth (1881 - 1952) had retired in 1936 but was recalled to active duty in September 1938 and appointed Chief of the General Staff, serving until September 1941. In March 1940 he was concomitantly named Commander-in-Chief of the Armed Forces.

had to lie in bed for two weeks. My quarters were in the home of a Romanian university professor (a medical internist). The professor had directed a sanatorium in Vienna for more than ten years. Because he was born near Arad, which made him a Romanian citizen, he had been invited to be a professor at the University of Kolozsvár. Both his wife and his assistant/secretary were Austrians. Within the family they spoke German. When the professor heard that I was ill, he offered his medical help. For two weeks he had me drinking linden tea, the assistant bathed me in 104-Fahrenheit water, and his wife cooked special diet meals. Finally, at the end of two weeks, I passed three peppercorn-sized kidney stones.

While I was ill, the Romanian authorities hounded many Magyars out of Romanian territory. In response, the Hungarian government ordered the expulsion of notable Romanians from the new Hungarian territories. My host was one of those on the list, but as a result of my intervention, the commander of the Transylvania Occupation Forces deleted his name from the list.

I returned to Budapest for a week's recuperative leave, while my deputy stayed on in Kolozsvár for a few more weeks. The melding of Transylvania into the mother country had begun.

With the onset of procurement of military supplies in quantity, a tremendous workload fell on us, making it necessary for me to work 12-14 hour days. There were occasions when at midnight we were still conferring in one of the Commissions. Many Germans visited me, generals as well as civilians. I had no time to concern myself with military events elsewhere in the world.

Nevertheless, I could not avoid having a view of the sites of Germany's great western victories. In January 1941, at the request of Defense Minister Károly Bartha[48], I participated in his delegation's tour during which the Germans showed us the places of their successes on the western battlefields. We saw the results of the

---

48   See footnote 27.

capture of the Belgian Fort Eben Emael, the graveyard of British equipment at Dunkirk, the sunken ships, the long-range artillery firing on Dover, and part of the Atlantic Wall. We then went by train via Paris to Saarbrücken where at the station our parlor car was connected to that of von Rundstedt[49], German commander-in-chief of the western front. Minister Bartha went over to visit von Rundstedt and invited him to visit us. With one of his adjutants, he indeed came and while we drank some good Hungarian apricot brandy he told us, well past midnight, how he, in World War I, had served as a general staff officer at the headquarters of the German Carpathian Army, and that in Máramarossziget he had partied many times and with great pleasure to the accompaniment of gypsy music. By morning we had arrived at Berlin; the temperature was minus 4 Fahrenheit. We had an appointment to see Hitler in the Chancellery. First Minister Bartha went in to see him, then he introduced the rest of us, lined up in a row.

My impression of Hitler was of a man of medium height, somewhat pudgy, with dark blonde hair and sky-blue eyes, who moved about effeminately. I noted that the pupils in his eyes were not visible. His handshake was soft. When he stepped past me, I looked again and still did not see any pupils in his eyes. (Later a doctor explained to me that everyone has pupils, but that those of morphine addicts contract so much that they are hardly visible).

For the ceremonial dinner we were the guests of Luftwaffe General Kesselring[50], who entertained us, on behalf of Reichmarschall Goering, in the reception hall of the Air Ministry. I sat next to Luftwaffe General Udet[51], who drew clever caricatures of Kesselring and Bartha, who were sitting opposite us, on plates using charcoal.

---

49 Field Marshal Gerd von Rundstedt (1875 - 1953), one of Germany's most respected senior officers.
50 Generalfeldmarschall Albert Kesselring (1885 - 1960) was commander of Luftflotte (Air Fleet) 2 at the time.
51 Generaloberst Ernst Udet (1896 - 1941) was Master-General of Air Ordnance and Inspector-General of Fighter Aircraft from 1939 until November 1941, when he committed suicide.

In the evening we were invited to a theater, where the opera "The Merry Wives of Windsor" was playing. The next day we each made visits to offices that were pertinent to our own professional specialties. At noon we were lunch guests of General Fromm[52], Commander-in-Chief of the German Home Army, in the army officers' club. Fromm, citing the bravery of the Hungarian hussars serving in Frederick the Great's army, made a very friendly speech which very much surprised us all. Bartha, who was not an orator, expressed our thanks for the reception in just a few words.

After this, passing through Vienna, where the Wehrkreis[53] commander paid a farewell visit to Bartha, we returned home. Overall, our impression was that the Germans were preparing for war against the Soviet Union.

In my area of responsibility, the Germans were intensively seeking friendly relations. Under the leadership of a Lieutenant Colonel, they sent a war production liaison group to Budapest. First, they requested shipments of winter protective equipment such as felt-lined boots, ski equipment, as well as toilet articles for which our industry was quite well developed. Later they asked for the substantial expansion of the already existing shipments of food stuffs, vegetable oils and bauxite. The Germans then proposed a mutual assistance program as regards the production of artillery equipment (mainly parts). Becaused the value of shipments from Germany of coke, coal, machine tools, industrial raw materials and semi-manufactured goods did not equal the value of the above-mentioned Hungarian exports, Germany's indebtedness to Hungary kept growing. This situation prompted Prime Minister Teleki to arrange a trip for me to Berlin, through the intervention of Alfréd Nickl, president of the Joint Foreign Trade Commission. My assignment was to buy as much war materiel from the Ger-

---

52 Generaloberst Friedrich Fromm (1888 - 1945) commanded the Home Army from 1939 until his dismissal after the July 20, 1944 plot to kill Hitler. Fromm was implicated in the plot and arrested, tried by a tribunal, sentenced to death and executed.
53 Wehrkreis is translated as Military District.

mans as could be obtained. The plan was to offer a high price that could not be refused, and demand as much as possibly could be procured. This was one of my most unpleasant tasks in my life. The trip almost ended in a fiasco. Only when I made it known to the Germans that I could not return empty-handed did they promise that they would let us have some materials from their war booty. It was not Nazi policy to strengthen Hungary. Otherwise, my personal relationships with Luftwaffe General Becker[54] (Section chief in the OKW Military Economic Staff) and Ambassador Clodius[55] (Southeast Europe Economic Commissioner) were pleasant.

Later, beginning with 1942, the situation in the Joint Foreign Trade Commission became so tense that the negotiations were held in my office. We had to say no to the German demands (mainly for oil), and this could be justified only on the basis of our own military needs.

Despite the mounting difficulties, until the Italians entered the war there were no major problems in the Hungarian economic situation. We reached a confidential agreement with England that it would allow the goods that we needed from overseas to pass through the Straits of Gibraltar. As soon as Italy entered the war our overseas supplies of raw materials stopped. At this time I often thought about the study authored by General Thomas (former chief of the Defense Economy and Armaments Office).

---

54 Generalleutnant Wilhelm Becker (1897 - 1964) took over as head of the Defense Economy and Armaments Office from General Thomas (see footnote 34) in 1942.
55 Carl August Clodius (1897 - 1952) was a senior official of the Commercial Section of the German Foreign Ministry. He was captured by the Russians in Romania in 1944, and died in a Soviet prison camp in 1952.

VIII. Hungary's entry in the war

1941 was, for several reasons, a decisive year for the fate of Hungary. With the German attack on Yugoslavia, Hungary became isolated from the rest of the world and was delivered to the whims of Hitler.

The trouble in the Balkans started with Italy attacking Greece through Albania. The root cause was Mussolini's dream of world power. Germany, ostensibly to secure her southern flank for the campaign against the Soviet Union, called on Yugoslavia to conclude a friendship treaty and advised Hungary to do the same. The Yugoslav and Hungarian governments did in fact conclude such a treaty. The Prime Minister and Foreign Minister of Yugoslavia were in Vienna for the purpose of conducting negotiations with the Germans when a Yugoslav general named Simović[56], with encouragement from the Russians, toppled the government by means of a coup and prevented the conclusion of a friendship treaty between Yugoslavia and Germany.

Hitler, outraged at the turn of events, declared war on Yugoslavia. His armies needed to attack partly from Romania and Bulgaria, and partly through Hungary. Germany's request for passage of its troops through Hungary precipitated a grave crisis in the heart of the Hungarian cabinet. Prime Minister Count Pál Teleki was vehemently opposed to an attack on Yugoslavia. The military leadership, however, persuaded Regent Horthy to authorize the attack, prompting Teleki's suicide. In the end, under the pretext that Yugoslavia was in the process of dissolution, we marched into the Bácska region.

---

56   General of the Army Dušan Simović (1882 - 1962) was Commander-in-Chief of the Yugoslav Air Force at the time he led the coup. He was named Prime Minister in the new regime, but was forced to flee the country when Germany invaded Yugoslavia in April 1941.

The German attack subjugated the entire Balkan Peninsula, rescued the stalled Italian campaign against Greece, and occupied the island of Crete by means of a paratroop assault. The campaign lasted two months (April - May 1941) and delayed the attack on Russia until 22 June.

For Hungary, the German Balkan offensive signified a total economic isolation. Our last gate to the outside world (Turkey, Egypt, and the Near East) slammed shut, and the country was delivered to the mercies of Germany. Hungary lost its neutrality, at the price of regaining (partly peacefully) 3.5 million inhabitants of its former territory. On the other hand, it became involved, albeit reluctantly, in a war on whose battlefields three ideologies were in contest, and in which it had no vested interest nor strength to participate.

The German attack on the Soviet Union started on 22 June, 1941. At the outset of the campaign, heavy air attacks hit the most eastern highlands of Hungary and city of Kassa. In response to these attacks the Hungarian government, under the leadership of Prime Minister László Bárdossy[57] declared war on Russia. With the consent of the Regent, but without the knowledge of the Parliament, it directed our ambassador in Moscow, Kristóffy[58], to present the declaration of war. When the facts became known, my first thoughts were that it was Hitler's greatest error to declare war on the Soviets, but for Hungary to do so was outright sinful. Openly the German leadership did not even desire Hungary's participation.

From the Hungarian side, the attack began with two light divisions and a mobile army corps (consisting of one cavalry brigade and two motorized brigades) under the overall command of Lieu-

---

57   Dr. László Bárdossy (1890 - 1946) served as Prime Minister from April 1941 - March 1942. After the war he was tried by a People's Tribunal in Hungary, sentenced to death and executed.
58   József Kristóffy (1890 - 1969) was appointed Hungarian ambassador to the Soviet Union in 1939.

tenant-Field Marshal Ferenc Szombathelyi[59]. From this Carpathian Group, only the mobile corps[60] advanced to the River Don; the other units returned to Hungary shortly after the crossing of the border. By the end of the year, the mobile corps also returned, but with this campaign the fate of the country was sealed with finality.

The Russian war did not become a Blitzkrieg. The Germans reached that point where they needed help, and requested the Hungarian government, among others, to provide troops. In early 1942, Prime Minister Miklós Kállay[61] consented to the provision of one Hungarian army. It consisted of nine light divisions and an armored division, under the command of Colonel-General Gusztáv Jány[62]. The army was deployed south of Voronezh, along the River Don in a defensive position that extended more than 125 miles.

This army represented about one third of Hungary's armed forces, but - because of overall shortages of armaments - some of its equipment had to be supplied from units remaining at home. Since it would have taken one-and-a-half years to produce the equipment stripped from the home units, I orally and in writing counseled against the 2nd Army taking all our equipment. My counsel was rejected by the High Command. The Germans promised to fill the gap in the equipment of the army, but they did not keep that promise.

---

59 Colonel-General Ferenc Szombathelyi (1887 - 1946) was appointed Chief of the General Staff and Commander-in-Chief of the Armed Forces in September 1941. He was removed from command in April 1944, and after the war was handed over to the Yugoslavs for trial, where he was sentenced to death and executed.

60 Commanded by Colonel-General Béla Miklós (see footnote 38).

61 Dr. Miklós nagykállói Kállay (1887 - 1967) replaced Premier Bárdossy in March 1942, and served as Prime Minister until March 1944. He was removed from office at the insistence of the Germans, who arrested him and confined him in Dachau, and later Mauthausen, concentration camps. After the war he went into exile in the USA.

62 See footnote 43.

It is claimed that even though the Prime Minister himself viewed the 2nd Army sent to the Don as lost, he could not find an alternative plan. In the face of a firm belief in German leadership, particularly in leading Hungarian military circles, the government could not come up with a better plan than yielding gradually to German pressure.

Up to the fall of 1942 the situation did not look bad, and there was hope that the country would survive the storm. Despite my heavy workload, my interest in the military situation was so intense that I prepared a study on the expected objectives of the German high command. In this study, I condemned the African (Rommel) expedition, purely on military grounds, and the penetration of Russia beyond the Rive Don, as well as the scattering of German forces throughout Europe. It was my unstated opinion that peace treaties should have been concluded with Poland and France. I sent the study to the Military Review, but the censor did not permit its publication.

In October, heavy fighting commenced for the possession of Stalingrad. At the same time the offensive for the Caucasus began. In North Africa, Field Marshal Rommel's[63] advance stalled at El Alamein. Around this time, at the invitation of the German embassy, I met Luftwaffe General Becker (OKW Defense Economy and Armaments Office), who was visiting. Aiming at Goebbel's current propaganda, I asked Becker whether and when we could expect Rommel's army group to join up with the German Caucasus army group. "I hope you don't believe in such crazy stuff?" was Becker's surprising reply. It was after this that the German 6th Army's catastrophe began at Stalingrad, followed by the Russian breakthrough against the Italian 8th Army, and finally the commencement of the attack against the Hungarian 2nd Army as a result of which the army was virtually annihilated. After its defeat,

---

63 Generalfeldmarschall Erwin Rommel (1891 - 1944) led the German forces in North Africa until March 1943, when he was transferred back to Europe. He was implicated in the July 20 1944 plot to kill Hitler and forced to commit suicide.

the remainder of this army was used by the Germans for occupation duty purposes in deployments against partisans.

Returning to my job as Chief of the War Industry Group, I need to make the following observations. While keeping the defense industries producing, the execution of various anti-Jewish laws caused a lot of worries for me, but never interrupted the flow of production. The changes in ownership that had to occur did not result in problems. Where trouble was anticipated, the Cabinet made exceptions to the laws. All the industries and all the work force acted very loyally at all times. They viewed their work as a national duty, and in recognition of this they were exceptionally treated as regards the supply of food and clothing, relative to their income.

Our plant managers were charged with checking and assuring acceptable wage levels and adequate provisions for the workers. All personnel were under military discipline and judicial authority. In cases of malfeasance by the plant management, the Defense Minister or Chief of the General Staff, as the designated authority, would take any necessary steps, but no significant irregularities ever occurred.

During the fall of 1942, more and more impatient voices rose from the staff of the new Chief of the General Staff, Colonel-General Ferenc Szombathelyi. The concern was that the defense industry did not produce at a fast enough pace, and that the people were living too well, a situation that could provoke German intervention. I responded to these complaints in a report. The responsibility for the industries not being able to produce at a greater capacity lay with the former governments, which had been reluctant to sacrifice money for expansion. As regards the population being well-off, this attested to the success of the economic mobilization. This did not hinder defense production, and it was necessary to look after the workers so as to forestall grumbling.

Some points of my report were severely criticized by Szombathelyi. A heated exchange of words ensued, as a result of which I requested to be removed from my assignment and be given a command in the combat zone. The Defense Minister (Károly Bartha) denied my request, and it was only in July 1943 that I succeeded in obtaining a combat assignment. Meanwhile, on 1 April 1942 I was promoted to the rank of Major-General[64].

---

64 At the age of 46 years, Jenő Bor became the youngest general in the Hungarian Army at that time.

IX. Field command

In July 1943 I was appointed commander of the 12th Light Infantry Division[65]. The division was deployed to the rear of the German line that lay behind the Desna River[66], forming part of the Hungarian VIII. Army Corps (Lieutenant-Field Marshal Dezső László[67]) and was tasked with securing the area.

I set off from Budapest for my new command on 20 July 1943, on a furlough train, and we did not detrain until we reached Kiev. The Hungarian Army of Occupation had its headquarters there, and I reported to the commander, Colonel-General Géza Lakatos[68] and his Chief of Staff, Major-General Elemér Mészöly[69]. After my briefing I went sightseeing in Kiev. The center of the town lay largely in ruins, although it was the retreating Russians who had blown it up. The headquarters staff of a German division had been the target of this act. The one notable thing that I remember is that in the Kiev cathedral's burial vaults I found the tomb of a prince of the Royal Hungarian house of Árpád, although I no longer remember his name.

---

65 Based on orders of battle, General Bor was actually named commander of the 4th Light Infantry Division, but was transferred to the 12th Light Infantry Division on 10 August 1943.
66 In the Ukraine.
67 Colonel-General Dezső László (1893 - 1949) commanded the VIII. Army Corps between May 1943 - April 1944. Later in 1944 he served as Deputy Chief of the General Staff, and until the end of the war as C-in-C of the Hungarian 1st Army.
68 Vitéz Géza nemes csikszentsimoni Lakatos (1890 - 1967) commanded the Army of Occupation until August 1943, before taking over command of the 2nd Army and then the 1st Army. Between August 1944 and October 1944, he served as Prime Minister of Hungary.
69 Elemér nemes sarbogardi Mészöly (1898 - 1980) was later Chief of Staff of the 2nd Army (until May 1944), a Bureau chief at the Ministry of Defense, and Secretary-General of the Supreme Military Tribunal. His last active command in the war was as commander of the 16th Infantry Division.

From Kiev I drove to Chernigov; the road was paved with cobblestones. In Chernigov was the headquarters of the Hungarian VIII. Army Corps under General László. After reporting, I continued to a village named Cholmy (about 25 miles east of Shchors) where the headquarters of my division was located. The division consisted of the 36th and 48th Infantry Regiments, an artillery component with Belgian batteries, as well as minimal support units. There was no great partisan activity in the division's area. The population was occupied with the harvest. The two regiments were deployed in defensive formation along the rail line.

Chernigov used to be the seat of a bishopric. Under the Communists, the bishop's palace, seminary, and the monastery were full of proletarian occupants, and the church was used for storage. There was no sign of religious life. In contrast, the little village of Cholmy had an undamaged church and services were held on Sundays. The priest looked like an old bell ringer, and only the women entered the church; the men stood outside and talked. The men acted the same way on holiday afternoons when the village girls danced; the men just stood around and smoked their cigarettes but did not dance.

The Russian offensive against the German front at the end of July pushed the line back. As a result, the area to be secured by the Hungarian divisions was also pushed further back. My division's new area of responsibility became the Bobruysk-Osipovichi region. We moved by rail, and the entraining station was at Shchors. The division command staff waited in Shchors for two days for its train. Here, some of the women coming from the rail-yard machine shop greeted me in Hungarian. In response to my questions they said that they were the wives of Hungarian soldiers. I ordered the legal officer on my staff to investigate the situation. It transpired that several marriages had taken place; the couples appeared in the infirmary of a signals corps unit stationed there, and entered their names in a large book whereupon the clerk declared them married. This was the story. When we left, divorces should also have been declared, but this only happened later because the "wives" followed their "husbands" and became laundresses and cooks' assistants in the unit.

Before we entrained a man came to me and said that he was Hungarian and requested that we take him and his family (a wife and two older children) to Hungary. We prepared a petition and submitted it through official channels to the Minister of Interior. While we awaited the decision we took the family with us. The son had been taught Hungarian by his father, but the daughter spoke only Russian as did her mother. Later I found out that there were several such situations.

Our trip took several days and we arrived in Bobruysk around 20 August. Here I was designated the VIII. Army Corps deployment chief in the area. My Chief of Staff at this time was Captain Iván Madarassy. In my capacity, I was to take over the area and duties of a German police division. The German division commander, General Pilz[70], was a man of average ability. His leadership consisted of administration without much thought. He was worried that soon his unit would become part of the front line, for which he did not consider it fit. The transfer of responsibilities went very slowly. The corps commander and the bulk of the 12th Division arrived only at the end of August. In Bobruysk, aside from the headquarters of the VIII. Army Corps, there was a German Ortskommandantur (town command) and an SS training regiment. The town commandant was General Staff Colonel Bachmayer[71] (a former Austro-Hungarian general staff captain). The town had a fort dating from the Napoleonic era, for the defense of the bridge over the Berezina River. The town was full of German supply and other support units. Normal civilan life continued.

As the rail cars of the 12th Division rolled towards Osipovichi, they passed corpses all along the rail line. During the night there was

---

70 Generalleutnant Rudolf Pilz (1888 - 1975) commanded the 203rd Security Division until August 1944.
71 Oberst Josef Bachmayer (1887 - 1957) ended the war as Chief of Staff of Wehrkreis (Military District) XVII.

an almost continuous firefight around the town. Osipovichi lay on the main line to Minsk, and therefore the partisans had ample reason for causing trouble. We needed to be prepared for serious opposition.

My first order was to desist from firing at night, and frequent patrolling during the day. For a while the partisans remained quiet. To the difficult situation was added the fact that the Germans were commandeering food, which turned the local population against them. Here I became very familiar with the partisan problem.

It took a month to deploy along the rail line and the road. We conducted a number of sweeps into the countryside, but without significant results. One day a soldier from our rail unit disappeared. Three days later he returned and reported that he had been kidnapped from a field and taken to a forest camp where he was interrogated under the leadership of a "general". In the end they let him go, saying that they had no bad intentions towards the Hungarians, but we should not bother them.

One night the partisans attacked and destroyed 200 yards of the rail line north of Osipovichi, in the sector controlled by the 36th Regiment. Two nearby emplacements were tied down under intense fire and since there were no reserves for a counterattack, little could be done. Nevertheless the defenders' fire caused substantial losses.

Next day the division surgeon reported that the Russian doctor of the small local hospital and his wife had been kidnapped. The Russian hospital patients remained without care and one of the surgical patients was screaming in pain. The surgeon asked permission for the Hungarian doctors to look at the patients. The Hungarian surgeon opened up the screaming patient's stomach, a potful of pus was drained, and the patient was able to leave three weeks later, healthy.

The Russian doctor had been taken to the camp of the partisan general to treat the many casualties from the rail line attack. For another month nothing happened.

During this time another partisan leader, in the pay of the Germans, burst into my headquarters demanding that we give him 2,000 rations of bread. I happened to out on inspection at the time. The assignment of this particular partisan group was to pacify the area north of the deployment of my division. After he received his bread from the Germans, he and his band swept out of town.

Suddenly I had a kidney-stone attack and was flown by plane to our hospital in Bobruysk. During the flight over the area controlled by the aforementioned partisan leader, I saw many villages on fire. He dealt radically with his compatriots.

From the hospital I was flown to Budapest. There, in the officers' hospital on Alkotás Street, within two days I passed a stone. After a week's rest I flew back to my army corps which by that time had moved to Pinsk, while the divisions were also in transit to their new deployment in the Pripyat Marshes area. Our new area encompassed the towns of Luninets, Stolin, and David Gorodok, in Eastern Poland. For a while things were quiet. From Pinsk I travelled by night-train to Luninets. On the way the engine hit a mine, but aside from being delayed nothing serious happened.

In the new area our Army Corps was put under the command of the 2nd German Army. The army commander was General of Infantry Weiss[72], and his chief of staff was General Staff Colonel von Tresckow[73]. The German formations and supply units in the area behind the 2nd Army were under the command of a General whose

---

72 Generaloberst Walter Weiss (1890 - 1967) commanded the 2nd Army between February 1943 - March 1945. In the final months of the war he commanded Army Group North and Army Group East Prussia.

73 Generalmajor Henning von Tresckow (1901 - 1944) was a principal participant in the July 20 plot to kill Hitler. When the plot failed, General von Tresckow committed suicide by blowing himself with a grenade, near Bialystok.

position was equal to a corps commander[74]. He was also headquartered in Pinsk and was on good terms with the commander of the Hungarian army corps. We were his dinner guests on several occasions.

The Hungarian artillery units (both field and anti-aircraft) were planning a modest St. Borbála feast[75]. We felt obliged to invite the Germans, with the two corps commanders as official honorary guests. As the ranking artillery officer, I was the host. In my dinner speech welcoming the guests, I mentioned that neither of them was an artillery man and proposed that we induct them as auxiliary volunteer (hilfswillige) artillerists. My proposal caused great joviality and was accepted. After this, General László went on leave and I took over command of the Army Corps for three weeks. During this time General Jenő Sövényházi-Herdiczky[76] commanded the 12th Division.

During this period between the middle of November and December 6, the Soviet forces continued to attack northeast and west of Kiev. Because of this, the Hungarian 18th and 19th Light Infantry Divisions which were securing the Zhitomir-Mozyr rail line were pulled back. On 6 December the 19th Division attached itself to the southern flank of the 12th Division (between Stolin and David Gorodok). The main body of the division stood in the area of Sarny.

On Christmas Eve it was reported to me that behind the front lines the Red (Soviet) partisans and the Ukrainian National Partisans were engaged in a battle with each other. Our area had three separate operating partisan groups: the Ukranian National, Pol-

---

74 Kommandant des rückwärtigen Armeegebiets 580 (Korück 580), assigned to the 2nd Army, was Generalleutnant Kurt Agricola (1889 - 1955), who held this command during 1941 - 1945.
75 St. Borbála is the patron of artillerymen, whose feast is celebrated on December 4.
76 Lieutenant-Field Marshal vitéz Jenő Sövényházi-Herdiczky (1892 - 1968) served with the VIII. Army Corps during 1942 - 1944 and ended the war in command of the Hungarian SS Division "Hungaria".

ish National, and the Soviet partisans. The Hungarians were on good terms with the Ukrainians. The Polish partisans were afraid to fraternize with us[77] because of the Soviets. The Soviet partisans attacked wherever they were able, and when they moved it was a sure sign that the Soviet Army would also attack shortly.

I ordered the 12th Division to strengthen its southern wing and to increase reconnaissance patrols. I instructed a general staff officer from the corps headquarters operations staff to reconnoiter by plane the area south of the Pripyat River. He did not report anything significant, but according to German intelligence a Russian attack could be expected in the beginning of January.

I wanted more reconnaissance, and to this end I entrusted Captain Vince Tisza of the 12th Division's command staff to make contact with the Soviet partisans secretly, and negotiate with them so that they would not move against Hungarian troops. As a result, we established that we were facing Red partisans all the way to the Bug River, but we were unable to reach an agreement with them.

According to Captain Tisza's report, the partisans, who were fighting for the interests of the Soviets, made a very military impression except for their clothes which were civilian. Among their weapons were the same machine pistols as used by the Red Army; they had written regulations the same as the military, and all had personal identification documents.

On 8 January 1944 the Russian offensive started at Sarny (against the center of the 19th Division), resulting in the division, which was securing an 85-mile stretch of rail line, being pushed back. My corps southern wing (12th Division) became exposed. The Russians, however, pressed only in a westerly direction and not towards the 12th Division to the north. I myself reconnoitered this fact using an armored train.

---

77   Despite our centuries-long friendship with the Polish people.

According to the agreement reached between the Hungarian and German governments, Hungarian troops were not to be deployed against the regular Russian army and, since such a situation was now developing, I had to take some measures. I reported the situation to the commander of the German 2nd Army and requested that he deploy German troops to secure the gap that had formed in the lines. General Weiss replied that he was aware of the situation, but because of a lack of forces he was unable to do anything. As a result, the southern wing of the VIII. Army Corps gradually became undefended over a 60-mile stretch.

On 10 January, Lt.-Field Marshal László returned from leave and I again assumed command of the 12th Division. It was at this time that I met an old acquaintance from Nagyvárad, Colonel vitéz Géza Sályi, who had just been appointed commander of the 36th Infantry Regiment. Until the end of February only minor actions took place with no significant results. The Russians were attacking only in a westerly direction.

To return to my stay in the Pinsk area, it was here that I first experienced the full measure of the German policy towards the Jews. When in Berlin in 1937, I had seen only that the Jewish shops were marked. In Pinsk, however, the Germans literally exterminated several thousand Jews. In the center of Pinsk all the Jewish houses were empty, and the synagogue was dynamited and in ruins. At the same time it is true that the residence of the Catholic bishop of Pinsk and a large monastery were also empty, but it may have been simply that the inhabitants had fled. The fate of the Jews, however, was revealed to me - unexpectedly - by a German SS Field Police officer.

We were dinner guests of the rear area commander of the German army corps. The dinner turned into a champagne-fuelled carousal. After midnight, when I saw that everyone was drunk, I wanted to leave. At the door a police officer stopped me and begged me to hear him out. He was completely drunk, and would not let go of me. He told me that he was unable to sleep. He had just been notified that his business in Hamburg had been bombed out by the British and, along with most of his family, he had lost everything he owned. But something much worse was that on the orders from higher above ("the Führer's order") he had to execute more than seven hundred Jews: men, women, and children. This is why he could not sleep - his thoughts dwelt on this all the time, and he was having terrible apparitions... I could not help him.

From the beginning of March 1944 I was on leave in Budapest. I was there on the 19th when the Germans occupied Hungary. Hitler had invited Regent Horthy, together with the Minister of Defense, Foreign Minister, and the Chief of the General Staff, to Berchtesgaden and, while they were there, German forces rolled into Hungary from the south and west. Horthy wanted to abdicate, but Colonel-General Szombathelyi persuaded him not to. The Hungarian armed forces were ordered by telegram not to resist. This order was a great mistake, and I and my friends were much saddened. The rounding up and deportation of Hungary's political leaders by the German Gestapo now began.

While I was in Budapest I received news of my appointment as commander of the VIII. Army Corps, as Dezső László's successor. Before my return to the front lines, on 23 March I requested an audience with Colonel-General Szombathelyi. He received me amicably and praised my performance on the battlefield. I, however, posed the question of what I should tell my troops about the shameful German occupation of Hungary. The answer was startling, "The Germans are correct in as much as they do not permit any disturbance to occur behind the front lines. The question will be solved politically. Your task is, however, to carry out orders and not to meddle in politics...".

This answer did not satisfy me. In my mind I prepared myself to withdraw the entire army corps back to Hungary, even against the opposition of the Germans. The VIII. Army Corps was by now in Brest-Litovsk. I flew there first, then to Kobrin to bid goodbye to my former division. The 12th Division was already preparing to take over part of the front line. The old prohibition that Hungarian troops were not to be used against regular Russian fighting units was no longer in effect.

The corps was renamed the II. Reserve Army Corps, and was comprised of the following divisions: 5th Reserve Division (commanded by General László Szabó[78]), 12th Reserve Division (commanded by General Béla Németh[79]), and the 23rd Light Infantry Division (General Jenő Sövényházi-Herdiczky[80]). For a while, the 53rd Infantry Regiment and 19th Artillery Group[81] were also under my command. The artillery of the 12th Division was given eighteen Goering howitzers and assigned for combat use to German VIII. Army Corps (General Hoehne[82]). Together with the outgoing corps commander, László, I visited the commander-in-chief of German Heeresgruppe Mitte (Army Group Center), Field Marshal Busch[83], in Pinsk, and also the commander of the German 2nd Army, Colonel-General Weiss. Busch's chief of staff was General Krebs[84].

Because of the 19 March events, the German units behaved insultingly toward Hungarian units. I protested to Field Marshal Busch,

---

78   Major-General vitéz László Szabó (1895 - ?) was commander of the division until February 1945.

79   Major-General Béla nemes felsözsidi Németh (1892 - 1968) commanded the 12th Division until the end of September 1944. His last command of the war was the 24th Reserve Division.

80   See footnote 76.

81   Both these units were assigned to the 19th Reserve Division.

82   General der Infanterie Gustav Hoehne (1893 - 1951) led the VIII. Army Corps between July 1943 - September 1944. He then commanded LXXXIX. Army Corps until the war's end.

83   Generalfeldmarschall Ernst Busch (1885 - 1945) commanded Heeresgruppe Mitte until June 1944, when he was transferred to the reserve. He was recalled in March 1945 to be C-in-C Northwest for the last months of the war. He died as a POW in England just a couple of months after the war ended.

84   General der Infanterie Hans Krebs (1898 - 1945) became the last Chief of the Army General Staff in April 1945. He committed suicide in Berlin at the beginning of May when the city fell to the Soviets.

who gave me satisfaction in the form of an Army Group General Order in which he directed the units under his command to behave honorably toward the Hungarian units.

At the end of March, the 19th Division got into a serious engagement with Russian forces which had advanced westward from Sarny. Southwest of Kovel, a Russian cavalry division attacked the defensive positions of the 53rd Infantry Regiment. Because of the very high casualty rate (40%), I inspected the position of Colonel Lupkovich and the batteries of Lieutenant-Colonel Filipovich. The commander of the battle group was a German armored forces Colonel, who received me and praised the Hungarian troops. The reason for the heavy losses was that the German Colonel ordered a counterattack into a wooded area, which stalled in the swampy terrain.

In April, the German 2nd Army took up positions between Vladimir Volynskiy and Luninets along the Bug and Pripyat Rivers. Both sides of the Kovel-Brest Litovsk rail line were defended by the German VIII. Army Corps, with the Hungarian 12th Division on its northeast wing. The Hungarian 5th Division was securing the Bereza-Kartuz rail line, while the 23rd Division, with one regiment in Brest-Litovsk, secured the Pinsk rail line. These changes in positions occurred during engagements with the enemy. It was only in the so-called Five Lakes region that there was any significant fighting.

With the front being pushed westwards, the strength of the partisans increased very substantially. They encamped in strength mainly in the forests of Niechoczevo, mounting continuous mining attacks against the Pinsk-Kobrin rail line which was a main supply line. Moreover, they kept the Drogitchin-Bereza road closed. This diagonally-cutting road was needed for tactical moves. Our offensive, in regimental group strength and with the 23rd Light Division's commander in charge, lasted from 6 April to the 15th. All rivers were very much flooded, and the bridges in ruins. The partisans had fortified the area between Lake Chernoe and Lake

Sporoyskoe and were defending it with machine guns. They repulsed our first attack, and the Corps commander ordered a repeat assault. The partisans, however, retreated on their own initiative. Our losses were several dead and wounded. The troops opened several fresh graves in the woods and found arms and ammunition in them. The partisans, as well as the inhabitants of the villages, disappeared; there were no prisoners taken.

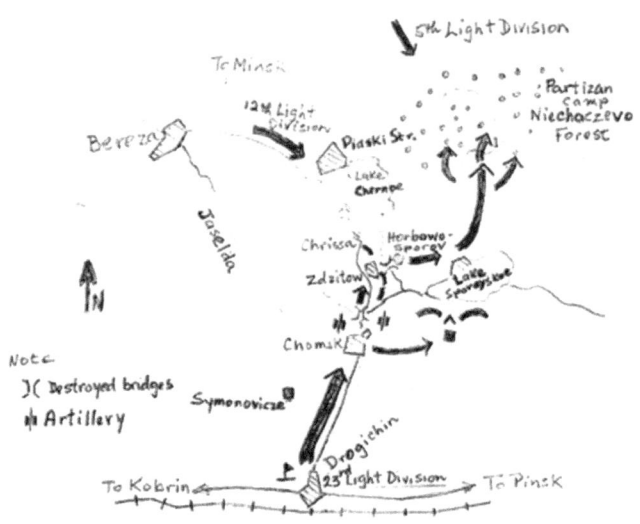

In April, the commander of the German 2nd Army invited me to a conference in Janow-Podlaski. Four German corps commanders were also there, and gave reports on their new situations. The commander of the XX. Army Corps (General Roman[85]) wanted to withdraw one of his battalions from a superfluous bridgehead located south of Luninets. He had requested permission to do this a month previously, because this battalion would have been his only reserve, but to date he had not received an answer. The army's chief of staff, General von Tresckow, called Army Group HQ, but the answer was in the negative.

---

85   General der Artillerie Rudolf Freiherr von Roman (1893 - 1970) led the XX. Army Corps for a large part of the war, September 1942 - April 1945.

After lunch I told General von Tresckow how surprised I was about General von Roman's situation, that a corps commander could not himself make such a decision! I would not have asked permission from a higher command. General von Tresckow enlightened me concerning Hitler's order that without his (Hitler's) permission not even a squad may be withdrawn. I said that I could not cooperate with them on such a basis, that my sphere of authority was not limited to such an extent. General von Tresckow replied that no matter what orders I might receive from them, I should always do what is best in my judgement. "Your Head of State is a rational person…". I left the conference knowing that we were left to our own ingenuity; we could not expect any help, nor permission to take advantage of the best of the available defense options open to us.

On 1 May, the new chief of staff of the army corps, General Staff Lieutenant-Colonel Károly Vasváry, arrived. The same day we were subject to our first large-scale night bombing attack. The attack came in five waves, but no Hungarian lives were lost and only a few vehicles were damaged. In our sector all doors and windows were shattered. The Germans diverted the enemy bombers by lighting some misleading fires.

In order to have the army corps command post located more centrally, I had it moved to Kobrin. From here I could reach the positions of the 12th Division more easily. My major concern was the completion of the outfitting of the 12th Division. To this end I even ordered some road construction. I pressed for the speed-up of training, and inspected the division twice a week.

At the same time, in view of an expected major offensive by the Russians, I had the corps materiel support (supply depots and other support units) moved back as far as the area between the Bug and Vistula Rivers.

Because the defensive positions of the 12th Division were not continuous, partisans moved back and forth between the gaps. In June, a group about 400 - 500 strong started to move through the line, acting on Russian orders. Their crossing of the Pripyat River in early morning was discovered by the Hungarian artillery, who fired upon the group and smashed it to pieces. In view of the failed attempt, the Russian command infiltrated punitive squads through the lines to execute for treason some of the "Starostas" (village leaders). Of the five who were so punished, one did not die, but with a neck wound reported to a Hungarian first aid station where he was treated; he recovered shortly thereafter.

To celebrate the Regent's birthday on 18 June, I had a ceremonial dinner prepared in the Corps' dining room. In addition to the Hungarian division and other unit commanders, I also invited the commanders of the German army group and 2nd Army. Field Marshal Busch appeared in person, but the commander of the 2nd Army sent General von Tresckow in his stead. I called to Busch's attention that according to custom, after the brief ceremonial toast to the Regent there were not to be any further speeches. Busch requested me to make an exception in his case because he thought highly of Horthy and had met him in person on several occasions. I could not refuse, and Busch made such noble comments about Horthy in his speech that it was a pleasure to hear his words.

On 24 June 1944 the Hungarian Cavalry Division[86] (later renamed the Hussar Division) arrived by train transport in the area of the Corps. It was positioned in Luninets and in the area north of the town, as the reserve of the German 2nd Army. At the same time, for training purposes, it was used against the partisans.

Around 28 June the Soviets mounted a strong attack against the 12th Division. The Division - and particularly the 48/I Battalion - repelled the attack with heroic defense. Only German artillery supported the Division's fight. After the battle, a German battalion took over the defense sector of one of the Hungarian battalions on the right wing.

---

86   The Division was commanded by Lieutenant-Field Marshal Antal Vattay (1891 - 1966).

On 6 July, the Soviet offensive pierced the German line and reached the little town of Slutsk. The Hungarian Cavalry Division (with the exception of the 2nd Hussar Regiment) was ordered to counterattack in a northeasterly direction. The Division became embroiled in heavy fighting. It was encircled three times, and twice it broke out by its own efforts. The third time a German armored division gave assistance. By this time the Hungarian 5th Division was being readied to back up the Cavalry Division, but this became unnecessary because the Soviet offensive let up for a few days. The Cavalry Division became totally exhausted by 12 July, having suffered losses that exceeded 50%.

When the Cavalry Division had arrived at the front, it had been subordinated to the German I. Cavalry Corps, under General Harteneck[87]. Serious differences of opinion developed between the commander of the Cavalry Division, Lt.-Field Marshal Vattay, and General Harteneck regarding the direction of military operations. These differences deteriorated into personal animosity. I found out about this situation (after the Division's third breakout) from the German liaison officer assigned to the Cavalry Division, who requested my intervention. I wrote a letter to Colonel-General Weiss in which I requested an investigation into the situation and the earliest withdrawal of the Cavalry Division, for rest. Weiss promised me that an investigation would be made, and did indeed withdraw the Cavalry Division from the front lines for 2 - 3 days. The Division rested in the region east of Kamieniec-Litewski.

As a result of the Soviet penetration my Corps had to redeploy, since our rail guarding mission was over. To fill the gaps created in the German line, we received orders to deploy in defensive positions north of Brest Litovsk. This plan, however, was upset by the breakthrough of a Russian cavalry unit and the Corps was forced to move behind the Bug River where, to the north of Brest Li-

---

[87] General der Kavallerie Gustav Harteneck (1892 - 1984) led the Cavalry Corps until the end of the war.

tovsk, the 23rd Division, then the 5th Division, and on the extreme left wing the Cavalry Division prepared for defense.

At this juncture I was ordered to fly home on orders from Budapest, and Lt.-Field Marshal Vattay, as the senior officer, took over command of the Corps. The new commander, not yet being familiar with the Reserve Corps units, requested that I stay with him for a few days. During this time the Corps HQ was transferred to Janow Podlaski and its connection with the 12th Division was broken.

On 18 July, the aforementioned Russian cavalry group broke through to the Bug River north of Janow Podlaski. Its columns were bombed for several hours by German Stuka bombers, but despite this it was able to reach the river and establish a small bridgehead there. The Hungarian divisions were still in motion and there were no other units available except for the engineering company of the Cavalry Division and the Corps HQ company. I threw these units against the Russian bridgehead. Meanwhile, a German militia battalion, on its march westward, arrived, and I requested its commander to stay with his unit until I was able to direct more Hungarian troops here. In the early morning hours of the next day a Hungarian battalion arrived. During the night I had moved the headquarters back to Miedzyrzec, where we took up quarters in one of Count Potocky's manor houses. The 5th Division's HQ, on the other hand, moved into Janow Podlaski. Lt.-Field Marshal Vattay returned to the 5th Division and ordered an attack on the Russian bridgehead. The attack failed, which caused the newly-appointed commander of the Division, General Győző Árvay[88], to have a heart attack. Consequently, the former commander of the Division, General László Szabó, resumed his command.

In the morning of 20 July, General Hoehne, commander of the German VIII. Army Corps, and his chief of staff rolled into my command post, muddy and exhausted, asking for my help. They

---

88   Major-General Győző Árvay (1890 - 1950) did not return to active duty after his heart attack.

related that a small unit of Soviet armor had broken up their headquarters unit and they had barely escaped. This had happened about 12 miles south from us. I deferred the question of aid for Hoehne to the German liaison officer. To secure my Corps' positions against a surprise attack, I sent out the engineering company from the Cavalry Division. For reconnaissance purposes, I sent out 1st Lieutenant Rozváczy with the remnants of a platoon of small armored vehicles. (This officer was later court-martialed and convicted by Lt.-Field Marshal Vattay for making a false report).

In the canteen, late afternoon of 20 July, the German liaison officer made a loud and condemnatory statement about the attempt on Hitler's life. At the same time he announced that General von Tresckow had become the victim of a partisan sniper attack. (Later it was revealed that von Tresckow had participated in the conspiracy against Hitler, and as a result of the failed plot had committed suicide).

The next day Vattay and I were invited to the combat positions of General von Roman, about 3 miles west of Miedzyrzec. Von Roman told us that the German VIII. Army Corps, the defending forces of the Brest Litovsk fortress (under General Felzmann[89], a former Austrian schoolmate of mine) and the Hungarian II. Reserve Army Corps (including the Cavalry Division) were now assigned to him. His task was to defend the shores of the Bug River on both sides of Brest Litovsk. He was going to bend the right wing of the VIII. Corps to the west, while the forces under General Felzmann and the II. Reserve Corps were to hold fast. The previous day Russian forces had broken forward in the direction of Lublin. The Hungarian 12th Division and the other units of the VIII. Army Corps were retreating westwards. Now that we had stopped the Russian attack from the north, we had to regroup against an attack from the south.

---

89   General der Artillerie Maximilian Felzmann (1894 - 1962) was a highly decorated officer who later was to command the XLVI. Panzer Corps and XXVII. Army Corps.

Vattay ordered the Corps' quartermaster unit to a point east of Warsaw, and the leanest possible command unit to the town of Losicze. I was preparing to go home, and was personally encouraged to do so by Colonel-General Weiss.

X. Recalled to Budapest

On 27 July I traveled by car to Warsaw, through the town of Siedlce. During the trip a German SS armored division (three tank battalions and three armored artillery batteries), with brand new equipment, was moving in the opposite direction. I was happy to see them going to the aid of the Hungarian II. Reserve Corps. (I later heard that this unit never reached our lines; it somehow disappeared the next day).

Because of a mistake, I had to wait in Warsaw for two days. I had a chance to tour the city and found the populace friendly. Then, on 29 July, I flew to Budapest. The next day was a Sunday, and I rested with my family.

On 31 July I reported at the Ministry of Defense, to Minister Csatay[90] and his deputy, Colonel-General Ruszkiczay[91]. Csatay received me warmly. He painted a sad picture of the situation and placed all his hopes in me to speed up the outfitting of units. He informed me that I would be the next Chief of the Main Materiel Group in the Ministry. The war materials industry had to be reorganized, and he considered me as the most knowledgeable in this area. I requested a few weeks patience so that I could assess the situation.

I was given the month of August on leave, which I spent with my family. In the evening of 1 August, I received a telephone call from the Foreign Ministry. They wanted to ascertain that I had

---

90 Colonel-General vitéz Lajos nemes csatai Csatay (1886 - 1944) had commanded the 3rd Army before being appointed Minister of Defense in June 1943. After the removal of Admiral Horthy as Regent, both Csatay and his wife committed suicide.

91 Colonel-General Imre Ruszkiczay-Rüdiger (1889 - 1957) served as Deputy Minister of Defense during February 1943 - October 1944. He was arrested by the Gestapo when the Germans overthrew Regent Horthy.

arrived home. Then I heard on the radio that an uprising against the Germans had started in Warsaw, led by a General Bor (it was the pseudonym of a Polish cavalry officer, Tadeusz Komorowski[92]). I finally realized why Colonel-General Weiss had pressed for my return home.

While I was on leave, a decisive event occurred on the southern flank of the Eastern Front. The entire Romanian army defected to the Russian side and with this opened the road for two complete Soviet Army Groups to break through in a westerly direction and thus, on the one hand to march into the Balkans, and on the other hand to encircle and roll up the German southern flank.

The Cabinet of Prime Minister Sztójay[93], which consisted principally of ministers friendly toward the Germans, decided in an extraordinary session to mobilize the Hungarian 2nd Army and the new 3rd Army[94], which consisted of only auxiliary divisions. The aim of these desperate measures was to occupy the passes in the southern Carpathian Mountains where we hoped to develop defenses against the imminent threat. The ensuing developments will be described below, however, the significance to me of the new situation was that in my new position a superhuman task awaited me.

Effective 1 September, 1944 the Regent promoted me to the rank of Lieutenant-Field Marshal and designated me as the new Chief of the Main Materiel Group (in the Ministry of Defense). At the same time he decorated me with the Hungarian Order of Merit, 2nd Class, with star and battle swords, for having saved the three

---

92 Division General Tadeusz Komorowski (1895 - 1966) was commander-in-chief of the Polish underground Home Army.
93 Colonel-General vitéz Döme Andor Sztójay (1883 - 1946) had served as Hungarian Ambassador to Germany between 1935 - 1944, before being appointed Prime Minister. He was executed by firing squad in 1946.
94 The 2nd Army was commanded by Colonel-General Lajos Veress (1889 - 1976), while the 3rd Army commander was Colonel-General József Heszlényi (1890 - 1945).

Hungarian Reserve Divisions from the collapse of German Army Group Center.

I oriented myself about the situation when I took up my position. The domestic industry was manufacturing only machine pistols and rifles, and ammunition for these. All other plants had been bombed out. The most serious problem was the equipping of the newly-mobilized 3rd Army. Materiel produced until now was destined for replacing the losses of the 1st and 2nd Armies, while virtually nothing was left for the 3rd Army. The monthly production capacity during 1942 - 1943 covered, on the average, the equipment for about one light infantry division. Overall, this was sufficient for the needs of the 1st Army which had deployed in the eastern foothills of the Carpathian Mountains in April 1944. After that, the enemy bombing started.

It was necessary to establish "mobilization equipment centers" because, as a result of the unsystematic and hurried mobilization in the past, equipment became mixed up. The 3rd Army's auxiliary divisions marched to the front with antiquated (World War I era) materiel, since this was all that was available.

Equipment centers were set up for the artillery in Hajmáskér, while those for the infantry were established in Várpalota, Zalaegerszeg and Jutas. The materiel that was stocked in various unit depots was transferred to the centers. The disadvantage was that the centers lacked sufficient trained staff and consequently the equipping of the units went slowly. There was also a great shortage in all sorts of equipment. Until the middle of October there were some shipments received from Germany, then even these stopped.

I inspected the quartermaster units of the armies and the equipment centers, and by 10 October I had an overview of the armed forces' materiel situation. It was very pitiful. I ordered General Staff Major Sóváry, my chief of staff, to prepare a situation report.

Since 23 August 1944, when it had capitulated to the Soviets, the Romanian army had been preparing, in conjunction with Russian forces, an attack on northern Transylvania and Hungary. The Hungarian 2nd Army, anticipating the Romanians, mounted an attack on 5 September but reached only Torda and the line of the Maros River; a strong Russian-Romanian counterattack threw it back. The 3rd Army with its weak forces also mounted an attack on 13 September, but only managed to reach Arad and the valley of the Fehér Körös River before a counterattack by the enemy forced it back to the borders of Hungary. Then, on 6 October, with overwhelming armored strength, the Soviet 2nd Ukrainian Front demolished the Hungarian 3rd Army, the remainder of which was pulled back to the line of the Tisza River by its commander. It was after this that the so-called "armored battled of Debrecen" began, and lasted until the end of October.

On the evening of 14 October, returning from my inspection tour in Zalaegersaeg I arrived at Balatonfüred, where my sisters were temporarily staying. The next day at noon I heard the Regent's radio address concerning the armistice[95]. Since the military academy (General Staff School) was also in this town in temporary quarters, I immediately went to see its commander, General András[96]. It was my understanding that the Chief of the General Staff of the Armed Forces, General János Vörös[97], was also visiting here, but he had already left.

With General András we concluded that a German intervention must be reckoned with and therefore, under my command, the stations in Jutas (the only one in radio contact with Budapest),

---

95   Admiral Horthy announced that Hungary was about to conclude a military armistice with the Russians, and would accordingly cease all hostilities against them.

96   Major-General Sándor András (1899 - 1985) was an air force officer who was actually Deputy Commandant of the General Staff School.

97   Colonel-General vitéz János nemes Vörös (1891 - 1968) had taken over as Chief of the General Staff from Colonel-General Szombathelyi in April 1944. He himself was replaced on 16 October, 1944.

Hajmáskér, Várpalota and Zalaegerszeg were put on the highest alert. With General Staff Major Kovács, I drove to Hajmáskér where the largest force was available and ordered an assembly of the officers. After briefing them, I requested that they voice their opinions. There were some who concurred with the Regent's decision, but there were others who did not. I reminded all of them about their officer's oath and ordered them back to their posts with the admonition that in case of need they should be ready to render assistance in the defense of the post.

General Billnitzer[98], who was in Budapest earlier in the day, returned to Hajmáskér around midnight. He had found out from Jenő Rátz[99], a former Minister of Defense, that the German Ambassador Veesenmayer[100] had demanded from the Chief of the General Staff, General Vörös, that he should order the continuation of fighting until negotiations were concluded. After this, I returned to Balatonfüred, where in the home of General András I heard the address by Szálasi[101] on the radio. Meanwhile, the Jutas station reported that a radio message had arrived from the Ministry of Defense, ordering me to report to Budapest. I reached Érd around 7:00 a.m. where, in thick fog, I ran into the first German roadblock. An SS Major did not want to let me pass. When I protested, he asked my name and then let me proceed.

First I went to my home, and from there to the Defense Ministry. On Castle Hill, in front of the Ministry, stood a battalion in for-

---

98   Major-General (later Lt.-Field Marshal) Ernö Billnitzer (1889 - 1976) was Commandant of Hajmaskér Field Artillery School.
99   Colonel-General vitéz Jenő nagylaki Rátz (1882 - 1952) had served as Minister of Defense for six months in 1938 before retiring. He was named Deputy Prime Minister in March 1944, serving until July 1944.
100 Edmund Veesenmayer (1904 - 1977) was appointed Reich plenipotentiary in Hungary in March 1944.
101 Ferenc Szálasi (1897 - 1946) was the leader of the fascist Arrow Cross Party, appointed Head of State of Hungary (by the Germans) on 16 October 1944, after the overthrow of Regent Horthy. After the war, Szálasi was tried by a Hungarian People's Tribunal, sentenced to death for war crimes and high treason, and hanged.

mation with each soldier wearing an Arrow Cross armband. There was hardly anyone in the Defense Ministry; I was finally able to reach by phone Kézay[102], the Chief of the Ministry's War Industry Group, who told me what had happened. Finally the new Defense Minister, Beregfy[103], arrived and notified me through his adjutant that he would call me later. Around noon, Secretary of State Szentgyörgyi[104] and I received orders to call all officers and civil servants to an assembly. Beregfy arrived and read a long statement. I hardly paid attention, but was thinking about what would happen as a result of this great turmoil. My battle front experience told me that the war was lost and I could not imagine what could be done to prevent this.

In the late afternoon of 16 October, Beregfy again called for me. In his office were General Staff Colonel Makay-Hollósy[105], his adjutant, and General Staff Colonel Miksa Bán[106], chief of the Defense Ministry's Operations Division. Beregfy asked me what my intentions were, for he could not get along without my technical knowledge in the fields of industrial mobilization and military supply management. I made references to my bad experiences on the front, that not so much our troops, but the Germans did not want to fight anymore. I also stated that I did not concur with the political views of the Arrow Cross Party. He responded that we soldiers do not get involved in politics, and that he intended to keep

---

102   Major-General Gyula Kézay (1893 - 1951) was named chief of the Group in June 1943 and served in that capacity until the end of the war.
103   Colonel-General Károly Beregfy (1888 - 1946) had previously been commander of the 3rd Army, 1st Army, and the Replacement Army before taking over the Defense Ministry on 16 October, concomitant with the positions of Commander-in-Chief of the Armed Forces and Chief of the General Staff. He was tried and executed in Hungary after the war.
104   Dr. Lajos nemes Szentgyörgyi was Chief of Group VII (Legal and Civilian Affairs) in the Ministry.
105   Colonel Ferenc Makay-Hollósy (1902 - 1986) served as Beregfy's adjutant from 16 October until the end of the war.
106   Colonel Dr. Mihály Bán (1900 - 1945) had been Chief of Staff of the 1st Army and the 3rd Army before his appointment to the Defense Ministry as Chief of Operations, later as Chief of Group II (Personnel).

me in my current position. To this I replied that "I will only be a burden to you, Mr. Minister," because he would be subjected to attacks on my account. He decided, however, that he would continue to entrust me with the leadership of the office of the Chief of the Main Materiel Group, and also designated me as his representative for economic ministerial conferences. I replied that if there was still some hope, I was willing to continue to serve. With this, my fate was once more decided. It is interesting to contemplate that a man's fate is always placed in the hands of others and never do we direct it by our own will.

Previously, at the front, it had happened to me that Colonel-General Géza Lakatos[107], then commander of the Hungarian 1st Army, had wanted me take command of the VII. Army Corps in place of General József Futó[108], who had been appointed to that position by the Defense Ministry. (Lakatos disliked Futó for personal reasons). This would have meant that Futó and I would have had to exchange commands. The Chief of the General Staff did not permit this change because General Futó did not speak German and the commander of the II. Reserve Army Corps - being in an isolated deployment (surrounded by German units) - had to know German. Thus I remained in my position. Now again, despite the fact that I condemned the political rule of the Arrow Cross Party, the Defense Minister insisted on my service. This is how, although only in appearance, I became an Arrow Cross supporter.

Returning to the events of 15 - 16 October, the situation was as follows: the Regent was abducted by the Germans and forced to abdicate. The commander[109] and Chief of Staff of the 1st Army crossed over to the Russians; the commander of the 2nd Army[110]

---

107 Colonel-General vitéz Géza nemes csikszentsimoni Lakatos (1890 - 1967) was named Prime Minister of Hungary in April 1944, and served until 16 October.
108 Lieutenant-Field Marshal József nemes Futó (1894 - 1967) commanded VIII. Army Corps until June 1944 and retired shortly thereafter.
109 Colonel-General Miklós - see footnote 38.
110 See footnote 94.

was arrested by the Germans; the commander of the 3rd Army[111], embroiled in heavy battles, remained in his post. The Chief of the General Staff, János Vörös, went into hiding.

Military and civilian political leaders who supported the Regent's plans for an armistice were systematically being arrested. Beregfy attempted to resist this wave, for example in the case of General Ruszkiczay-Rüdiger. The Kovarcz[112] Group rampaged throughout Budapest. Beregfy introduced a system whereby the Ministry's division chiefs met with him every morning and presented the latest updates. At such meetings questions arose regarding the consolidation of the position of Defense Minister and Chief of the General Staff, about summary court proceedings, the German request to meld Hungarian units into German units, and other related matters.

Reorganization of the armed forces was the paramount problem since, as a result of heavy losses, some units completely disappeared and new ones could not be raised on account of a lack of equipment. To exercise political pressure, politically reliable (Arrow Cross) units were to be established in the hinterland. I perceived my principal duty as supplying the fighting troops, and was unwilling to equip the Arrow Cross battalions. When Beregfy asked me why I treated the Arrow Cross units as secondary in importance, I replied, "there is not enough even for the fighting troops...".

At another meeting, Colonel-General Feketehalmi-Czeydner[113], who had become Deputy Minister of Defense, complained that

---

111   See footnote 94.
112   See footnote 114.
113   Colonel-General vitéz Ferenc Feketehalmi-Czeydner (1890 - 1946) had commanded V. Army Corps until August 1942 before retiring. Being strongly pro-German, he joined the SS (rising to the rank of Obergruppenführer) and was named Deputy Commander of the II. SS Panzer Corps. After the coup that overthrew Regent Horthy, he became Deputy Defense Minister until January 1945 when he went on sick leave (throat cancer). After the war he was tried and executed by the Yugoslavs.

it was impossible to make the Germans understand that Budapest should not be defended within the city, but from prepared defenses outside the city.

Szálasi expanded his cabinet by several ministers, most without portfolio. Among them was Emil Kovarcz[114], in charge of total mobilization, who butted into everything. At one meeting of the ministers on economic matters, he propounded that the regulations governing the acceptance of military goods by military personnel in factories should be made less stringent. I protested vehemently against this and labeled it as inappropriate, rejecting his request.

My most important task at that time was to put together a report assessing the overall materiel situation; my staff prepared this report. When it was finished, I wanted to present it to Beregfy, but he continually kept postponing our meeting. Then he finally decided that I should make the situation report to the entire cabinet, in Szálasi's presence. The cabinet meeting took place around 10 November; the head of Section 1 of the General Staff made his report on the military situation, followed by the chief of Group I of the Defense Ministry reporting on organizational matters; finally it was my turn to make my report on the materiel situation.

In my presentation, which lasted two hours, I enumerated, by item, the situation regarding existing supplies and their production situation, including German deliveries. At the conclusion of a report that described a rather pitiful scenario, I concluded as follows: "Since October 1944 the supply of military equipment to the armed forces has been minimal. German deliveries are much interrupted. The army is literally consuming itself. Of course, it is still possible to continue fighting, but the minutes of such resistance are numbered…".

---

114   Emil Kovarcz (1899 - 1946) was a former army major and the commander of the Arrow Cross militia. After the war he was tried as a war criminal, sentenced to death and executed.

After this, Szálasi started to speak. He thanked me for the presentation and said that the data could not be disputed. With that he dismissed us and asked me to follow him. In the office of the Deputy Minister of Defense he asked me, as someone who had recently returned from the front lines, what my experiences were. I told him that I could only speak about the second-rate three divisions of the II. Reserve Army Corps and the Cavalry Division, which was a first-class fighting unit. The infantry divisions, despite their poor equipment, had held their own. The excellent Cavalry Division had suffered grave losses during its 10-day heavy battle. It had lost most of its armored vehicles and its artillery. But the main problem was that the German troops were demoralized and did not want to fight anymore. The string had been stretched too far...

Szálasi thanked me for the briefing and stated that he had been assured by the Germans that the discipline of the German Army was excellent. I responded that they had hardly any infantry left. He then asked about my family's situation, and bid goodbye.

The following day a military judge subpoenaed by chief of staff in charge of methodology and detained him for two days. Later, a judge asked me about details concerning supply management. I refused to provide this information as this was strictly confidential and communicable only to my superior, the Defense Minister. As justification, the judge stated that a defeatist spirit permeated my staff, against which I vehemently protested.

Nothing happened for a while, but the battlefield situation continued to deteriorate. The Soviet attack had reached the southern tip of Csepel Island and the area around the towns of Monor and Pilis. The Defense Ministry evacuated to Farkasgyepü, in the Bakony Mountains. Until the middle of December we stayed in Buda. The Deputy Minister of Defense traveled to Germany for the purpose of discussing the evacuation of the Hungarian armed forces.

XI. The final months of the war

One day I went to Farkasgyepü from Budapest to make a report to the Defense Minister. It was at that time that Beregfy told me that he was reorganizing the Ministry again, and that my position would be terminated. On the basis of an agreement with the Germans, training units and still-available military supplies, raw materials and war industry would be transferred to Germany. The Commander-in-Chief of the displaced armed forces would be Colonel-General Jenő Major[115], the commander of the 2nd Army, and I would be the Defense Minister's Chief Commissioner for Materiel. A staff had been set up in Vienna under General Staff Colonel László Zsigmondy, to keep track of and direct shipments. Zsigmondy was placed under my command. This is how I wound up in Germany, with my family who accompanied me. I was assigned a small staff which consisted of a General Staff officer, an adjutant, a quartermaster, and a few technical experts. I left my adjutant, Lieutenant-Colonel Rudolf Voernle, in Vienna to serve as my liaison officer with Colonel Zsigmondy, and I, for the time being, took my staff to Prague. The bulk of materiel was directed to this area.

In Vienna, the Wehrkreiskommandant[116] was the German General Schubert[117]; his chief of staff was General Staff Colonel Bachmayer, my old acquaintance from Bobruysk. The Hungarian units there were commanded by General László Kesseö[118]. I entrusted the care of my family to my adjutant Voernle and left them in Vienna.

---

115   Colonel-General vitéz Jenő Major (1891 - 1972) took command of the 2nd Army on 16 October 1944.
116   Commander of a Military District.
117   General der Infanterie Albrecht Schubert (1886 - 1966) commanded Military District XVII from August 1943 until just before the end of the war.
118   Major General vitéz László Kesseö (1892 - 1952) had previously commanded the 1st Anti-Aircraft Artillery Brigade, before his appointment, in January 1945, as Hungarian commander in Military District XVII.

I had an interesting occurence in Prague. Czechoslovakia was a protectorate under German occupation. The military commander, General Toussaint[119], and the SS Police Chief were headquartered in Prague. The old Hungarian embassy had been transformed into a consulate. The Chief Consul was a hussar officer, an acquaintance of mine from Miskolc, who hosted a party in my honor inviting the German commander, SS Chief of Police, as well as the leading actors of the UFA film company who happened to be working in Prague at that time. It was here that I got to know General Toussaint, who had been military attaché in Budapest for a brief period. He told me that previously he had been the German Army Commissioner in Italy and gave a very scornful opinion of Mussolini. At the end of our chat, I asked him for an official appointment so that I could pay my respects. He set the time for the following day.

When we arrived in Prague, my staff and I were assigned quarters in an elegant hotel. At the evening meal, and even more so at breakfast, several very good-looking women sat down at our table and made a friendly offer of help to show us around town. After supper I warned my staff that these women were not tourist guides, but spies. However, we were unable to politely shake off these women.

Meanwhile, together with my chief of staff I visited the Chief Quartermaster of the military command who, according to my information, managed the logistics of the Hungarian materiel. I requested data on shipments from him, but he refused, stating that without permission from the Allgemeines Heeresamt[120] in Berlin he could not divulge anything. I attempted to contact the office in Berlin by phone, but could not get a proper connection. After my futile conference with the Chief Quartermaster, I threatened

---

119 General der Infanterie Rudolf Toussaint (1891 - 1968) commanded the Military District of Bohemia-Moravia from July 1944 until the end of the war. He was imprisoned by the Czechs until 1961.
120 The General Army Office was part of the Army High Command (Oberkommando des Heeres).

to call a halt to all further shipments from Hungary. This was reported to Beregfy, who interdicted my order.

In addition to paying my official respects, my visit to Toussaint had two main topics: the women spies and the incident with the Chief Quartermaster. I stated that on the Eastern Front I was a welcomed "Kamerad", while here I was being surrounded by spies. I requested that he call off the women, which he promised to do. They did not appear the next day. I also asked him to instruct his Quartermaster to provide me with the appropriate information. In response, after several phone calls, he asked me to go to Berlin where the Allgemeines Heeresamt would be at my disposal.

After all this, I traveled to Berlin where I reported to Jenő Major and told him about my experiences with regard to the materiel shipments. Colonel Zsigmondy had already assigned a liaison officer to the Allgemeines Heeresamt, Colonel Rudolf Frankovszky (a classmate of mine from Traiskirchen). Frankovszky had already reported German abuses in East Prussia where, retreating from the Russian advance, they had distributed the Hungarian materiel to German troops despite the protestations of the Hungarian commissioner, Lieutenant-Colonel Szilárd Zigury. The question was, how had the Hungarian materiel ended up in East Prussia? This characterized the state of complete confusion of the German railroads. The bombings had totally disrupted rail communications.

A large part of Hungarian units in training was shipped to Schleswig-Holstein and also to Denmark, and no-one could inform me of the whereabouts of the materiel. It had to be located by personal search. Of the approximately 24,000 rail carload shipments, not including barges on the Danube, we were able to locate only 7,500 cars. Naturally, we lodged strong verbal and written protests to the Allgemeines Heeresamt, however there were no significant results.

Since I was in Berlin, I looked up by good old acquaintance General Leeb[121], the chief of the Heeres Waffenamt. When I asked him about the situation, he replied precisely as follows: "Deutschland ist an den tiefsten Punkt ihrer Geschichte angelangt..." (Germany has reached the lowest point in its history). Later, I went to Potsdam to confer with the commander of the Arsenal (Zeugamt). In his office he spoke sparingly. He recommended a restaurant for lunch where, to our surprise, he himself showed up and poured his heart out. He told us, "Here everybody is lying; nobody dares to open his mouth; you should not believe anyone, no matter what they promise...".

I reported all my experiences to Colonel-General Major and we decided that I should travel to Kőszeg to brief Beregfy. At that time (the end of January 1945) the seat of government was in Western Hungary. After I received my travel permit from the Germans, I traveled to Kőszeg. Beregfy did not receive me for an entire day, which I spent with my family. On the following day I met with him, and spoke to him for an hour about the situation in Germany and told him that all competent persons considered the war lost. He took notes, but did not speak a single word on the subject. Finally he asked me when I was going to return. This was the result of my journey.

That evening I had supper with General Ferenc Deák[122], who was the chief adjutant of the National Leader, Szálasi. I repeated to him what I had told Beregfy. He asked me to delay my departure that was planned for the next morning, because he would get me a meeting with Szálasi. I promised that I would wait until 10:00 a.m. to hear from him, but would be on my way otherwise. I did not receive word, so I traveled back to Vienna, and from there to Berlin.

---

121 General der Artillerie Emil Leeb (1881 - 1969) headed the Waffenamt (Army Weapons Office) from April 1940 until the end of the war.

122 Major-General Ferenc Deák (1897 - 1949) was Chief of the National Leader's Military Office during October 1944 - May 1945. He was tried by a People's Tribunal after the war, and executed.

Materiel shipments continued to roll into Germany. According to Zsigmondy they were soon lost without a trace. Because of this, I decided to make an inspection tour. In late February or early March, together with my quartermaster, Major Lajos, I traveled to the Sudetenland (Éger and environs), where most of the depots contained quartermaster supplies. On 14 March I returned to Berlin, via Sonnenberg where I picked up General Staff Lieutenant-Colonel Károly Vasváry[123]. Here, because of the recent advance of the Soviets, we were virtually helpless.

Between 18 - 25 March, Beregfy came to Berlin in response to a German invitation. He visited Guderian[124], Jüttner[125], Keitel[126] and Himmler[127]. I participated only at one dinner where Keitel was the host and despicably denigrated the Regent, with Beregfy seconding him at times. Next to me sat General Staff Colonel von Tippelskirch, while opposite me sat Hitler's brother-in-law, an SS Cavalry General[128], who during the entire dinner discussed the new German cavalry saddle with his neighbor. After Berlin, Beregfy inspected the Levente[129] camp in Éger, then the war games of the Hungarian SS Division "Hunyadi" in Grafenwöhr. Not even

---

123 The author's former chief of staff on the Russian Front.
124 Generaloberst Heinz Guderian (1888 - 1953), a renowned Panzer expert, was Chief of the Army General Staff between July 1944 and March 1945.
125 SS Obergruppenführer Hans Jüttner (1894 - 1965) headed the SS Main Leadership Office, and after July 1944 was also acting C-in-C of the Replacement Army and Head of the Army Armaments Office.
126 Generalfeldmarschall Wilhelm Keitel (1882 - 1946) was head of the Armed Forces High Command (Oberkommando der Wehrmacht - OKW) from February 1938 until the end of the war. He was one of the main defendants during the Nuremberg Trials, where he was sentenced to death and hanged.
127 Heinrich Himmler (1900 - 1945) was named head of the SS (Reichsführer SS) in 1929, and retained this position until April 1945. He committed suicide when captured by the British after the war's end.
128 SS Gruppenführer Hermann Fegelein (1906 - 1945) served as SS liaison officer to Hitler's headquarters. As the Russians were closing in on Hitler's bunker in April 1945, Fegelein tried to flee but was arrested, charged with desertion and executed.
129 The Levente was a para-military youth training organization.

a quarter of the division had weapons or other equipment. Although the Germans promised the supplies shortly, we knew that nothing would come of it. Jenő Major reported this to the Defense Minister, but Beregfy replied that Major saw things too darkly.

By now the Hungarian government had left Hungarian territory and had settled in Semmering (Austria). It was at this time that I was conducting another extensive inspection tour in Lower and Upper Austria. The main military depots for vehicle parts, for road and bridge construction and rail supplies, weapons repair, and the central supply station were situated here. In Linz, where General Ankay-Anesini[130] was the Hungarian commander, I received the news of our total withdrawal from Hungarian soil. I hurried back to Vienna where everything was already in an uproar. I prepared my family for a further move.

The Germans had set up roadblocks where they stopped Hungarian refugees and disarmed military units. There had been armed clashes already between German and Hungarian units. Together with General Kesseö, we went to the commander of the Wehrkreis and I vehemently protested - in the name of the Hungarian government - against such conduct. To this General Schubert replied that he was no longer the commander but an SS General had taken over the leadership. While I was meeting with General Schubert, my automobile was confiscated while it was being refueled. I went to the office of the new SS commander, whose chief of staff listened to me and returned my vehicle. Concerning the roadblocks, however, he made no promises.

Reaching my quarters I ordered our departure for the next day, 2 April 1945, towards the area of Linz-Pyburg. The general evacuation of Vienna was also ordered for that same date. On our trip over the River Ems we came upon a German roadblock again, where a number of Hungarian - as well as German - units had

---

130   Major-General Győző Ankay-Anesini (1893 - 1955) had retired in February 1943, but was recalled in the final weeks of the war.

been stopped. It took a lengthy negotiation and dispute on my part to come to an agreement with the local commander. I left a small staff behind to direct the passage of legitimately retreating Hungarian units, and returned to Pyburg to spend the night.

After this, I took my family to Bayreuth, where my staff was also headed. Leaving my family in Bayreuth, Colonel-General Major and I drove to Berlin where I was going to report the events in Austria to SS General Jüttner, the head of the Army Armaments Office. I began my report with: "I was a witness to the Austrian collapse..." to which he replied with astonishment that he was unaware of this. I described what I had seen, that it was very much like my experiences in the final days of World War I.

Early in April, Jenő Major and I concluded that, on the basis of official situation reports sketched on the map, that Germany would shortly be sliced into two parts by the Allied forces. It appeared probable that the two attacking forces would meet somewhere south of Berlin. In light of this situation, we considered it necessary for the Hungarian units scattered to the north to be placed under a high-ranking commander who could direct their fate as long as the German command was still functioning. Later, when they had been captured, this commander would take the initiative in approaching the victorious powers. We visited Jüttner to find out the Germans' intentions.

Under the condition that General Major undertook the care of my family, I accepted the command of the Hungarian troops scattered in northern Germany. Major accepted this responsibility and headed south to confer with Beregfy. The Defense Ministry was now in a nunnery in the town of Metten, in the Bavarian Alps. Beregfy agreed to our proposal, and I was assigned a separate staff headed by General Staff Colonel Sándor Szávay[131] (who within a few days, through his friends in Metten, arranged to be redeployed

---

131 Colonel Sándor nemes Szávay (1900 - 1972) had been chief of the Defense Ministry's II. Bureau (Personnel) until the end of 1944, before his appointment as Chief of Staff to General Major.

south). Meanwhile, we came to an agreement with our ambassador in Berlin, András Mecsér[132], and our military attaché, General Staff Colonel Makray[133], that the war was lost.

Jenő Major left for Metten on 13 April. I asked Mecsér to provide me with a diplomatic certificate according to which I would be empowered to confer officially regarding military matters with the victorious powers. Having received the certificate, my staff and I left for Lübeck on 17 April. Along the way we were attacked from the air and one of our vehicles was damaged.

When I arrived in Lübeck I got in touch with Colonel István Vaska, who was the commandant of the armored school. In a personal letter, I gave both him and Lieutenant-Colonel Szilárd Zigury orders that they should not fight against the forces of the Western Powers. I found out that the commander of the northwestern German front, Field Marshal Busch, was headquartered near Hamburg, and I paid him a visit. He received me amicably as an old acquaintance from the Eastern Front. He had lost weight and gave me the impression of a completely broken man. He briefed me, "The Anglo-Saxons are advancing at a rate of 55 miles per day". He did not have enough forces to slow this advance. Only one third of his units had weapons - these fought in the front lines. Another third had personal equipment and shovels, and these constituted the reserves, but only as far as bodies were concerned. The last third did not even have personal equipment, so were being used to build transitory defensive positions. The Hungarian troops were included among these. He said that this was the beginning of the end, or even the end of the end. I asked him why he had accepted this impossible task, to which he replied, "If you were told by your head of state what Hitler had said to me, that all his confidence rested now only in you, what could you do?". I did not know how to reply.

---

132 András Mecsér (1883 - 1946) was appointed Ambassador to Germany in November 1944.
133 Major-General Sándor Makray (1898 - 1968) served as Military Attaché in Berlin from November 1944 until the end of the war.

Returning to Lübeck I found the city in terrible ruins. A church steeple with its huge bells lay in the street. People passing by either knelt down or stood and said a short prayer and then went on their way. It was rumored the Himmler was negotiating with Count Bernadotte[134] - the Vice-President of the Swedish Red Cross - in the matter of prisoner exchange.

New quarters were assigned to me in a military barracks in Flensburg (north of Lübeck). However, I wanted to go at all costs to Denmark because some 40,000 Hungarian troops were there. The Germans would not let me cross the border. I protested, in response to which the commander-in-chief of German forces in Denmark[135] gave me permission to cross with the proviso that I go to Roskilde where Colonel Vittay[136] (commander of a training regiment) would brief me. Afterwards, I was to report to the commander-in-chief of Silkeborg. My staff quarters were to be on the grounds of a German convalescent home near Aabenra.

Roskilde is situated about 20 miles west of Copenhagen. Colonel Vittay was waiting for me there, and together we crossed by ferry from Nyborg to Seeland Island. On the boat I was led to the first-class section where, during the trip that lasted several hours, I made the acquaintance of a distinguished-looking middle-aged couple. When they found out that I was Hungarian they became very friendly. He told me that he was the chief director of the Danish Railroads Center. I openly complained to him that the Germans had transported Hungarian troops into Denmark without the permission of the Hungarian government, which would likely spoil the heretofore friendly Hungarian-Danish relations. I told him that we were not in favor of this, and I had come here

---

134   Folke Bernadotte, Count of Wisborg (1895 - 1948) was the grandson of King Oscar II of Sweden.

135   Generaloberst Georg Lindemann (1884 - 1963) had commanded Army Group North in 1944 before being transferred to the reserve. He was recalled in January 1945 to become Armed Forces Commander, Denmark.

136   Colonel vitéz Béla Vittay (1897 - 1975) commanded the 93rd Training Regiment.

to regulate the behavior of the Hungarian troops toward the Danish population so that the good relations would not be harmed. I asked him to bring this to the attention of the Danish government, which he promised to do. (After we parted, I began to suspect that the person I had spoken with was actually Swedish Count Bernadotte).

After Vittay reported to me, we immediately proceeded, through heavy rainfall, to Copenhagen, to the Hungarian embassy. The new Hungarian ambassador was the younger brother of Baron Kemény[137], the Foreign Minister, who complained that the Danish government had not received him for six months. In fact, with the exception of the chargé d'affaires, they had not received any member of the embassy.

I requested the chargé d'affaires to inform any member of the Danish government about the situation, and to ask the government to provide a common shelter and provisioning for the families of the Hungarian troops, until they could be transported home. The fate of the soldiers themselves would be decided initially by the Germans, and - after the armistice - by the commanders of the Allies. In any event, we wished to withdraw from Denmark.

The staff of the embassy made a poor impression on me; an exception was the person in charge of propaganda, a young minister of the Reformed Church whose name I no longer recall. The staff looked to me for an improvement in their situation.

After this, I went to inspect Colonel Vittay's regiment. He reported that his units were being used to secure rail lines. There had been only one small incident, where a rail line had been blown up. The Danes did not engage in much partisan activity, and were friendly toward the Hungarians. Indeed, Colonel Vittay had been

---

137 Baron Gábor Kemény (1910 - 1946) was appointed Foreign Minister after the October 1944 overthrow of the Horthy government. He was tried by a People's tribunal and hanged after the war.

invited to their underground meetings. Vittay informed me that his propaganda officer (a Second Lieutenant) had asked to be relieved of his duties, and that no-one had volunteered to be his successor. I ordered the officer to report to me, and asked him why he had requested to be relieved of his duties. He candidly replied that he did not believe in the spirit of the Arrow Cross propaganda and could not work against his convictions. I commended him for his honesty and officially acknowledged his report. With this, the position of propaganda officer ceased to exist.

We then visited the headquarters of the local German commander, but did not learn anything significant from him. I bade farewell to Vittay, saying that he should keep a viable contact with the Danish underground - the war would end soon... From there I had myself driven to Silkeborg (northern Denmark), where the chief of staff[138] of the German commander-in-chief received me and was my host for lunch (the commander was ill). He told me that he had participated in the battles in Hungary and had been transferred from there to Denmark. (I later found out that he was the general who, pursuant to orders from General Johannes Friessner[139], commander of Army Group South, had arrested Colonel-General Lajos Veress, commander of the Hungarian 2nd Army). After my visit, I returned to my designated post near Aabenra to await the announcement of the armistice.

I received a report that in a school for reserve officers a mutinous mood reigned, and decided to make an inspection. The students (the bulk of them were officer-candidate sergeants) were demanding that they be transported home. I went to the school, gathered the students together and related to them the turmoil that reigned in Germany. Rail traffic was at a standstill, there was no food available, and the hostile powers overran large areas each day. We could

---

138   Generalmajor Hellmuth Reinhardt (1900 - 1989) took over as Chief of Staff to the Armed Forces Commander, Denmark, in January 1945.
139   Generaloberst Johannes Friessner (1892 - 1971) commanded Army Groups North, South Ukraine, and South during 1944, before transferring to the reserve in December of that year.

go home only on foot, which would last weeks, and we would have to carry our food with us. I told them that the war would be over soon, and when the armistice came I would make arrangements for us to be transported home. I warned them that they should also keep in mind the threat of becoming prisoners of the Russians. Finally, I instructed them that while we were here, they should trust in their superiors and maintain order and discipline. However, anyone who on his own initiative wanted to start heading for home was free to do so, as far as I was concerned. There were no volunteers…

XII. Armistice and captivity

On 8 May 1945, an armistice was finally concluded with the Western Powers. I immediately requested permission to proceed to British headquarters. Finally, on 10 May, I was able to leave, with a pass to cross the British lines. I took with me my personal adjutant, Lieutenant-Colonel Baldermann, who spoke French. We were able to reach Hamburg with hindrance, while in the direction opposite to ours strong armored forces were headed toward Denmark. At the northern entry point into Hamburg an officer-movement-control patrol stopped us and escorted me to the local English commander. I told him that my intention was to go the English commander-in-chief. He invited me to lunch and during lunch I related to him our situation and my plan. After lunch they seated me in a room to wait. In the afternoon a motorized patrol came for me and drove me to the area of Lüneburger Heide where Montgomery's[140] headquarters were located. Here a general staff officer received me, took from me the diplomatic certificate given to me by Ambassador Mecsér, and requested that I go to my quarters until they had time to deal with me. These quarters were in Lüneburg and were full of German generals. I had been transported to a generals' prisoner-of-war camp, amid some 170 German generals.

For a few days nothing happened, and during this time I wrote down the subject matters for negotiations. I described our situation - that the training units had been sent to Denmark without the knowledge of the Hungarian government - and requested that we be separated from German units. I called particular attention to the Levente units which had been melded into German units. I requested care for the families and earliest return home of the enlisted men. With regard to Hungarian officers, I requested (in

---

140 Field Marshal Bernard Montgomery (1887 - 1976) was commander of the Allied 21st Army Group, responsible for operations in Northwest Europe.

view of the rumored bad reputation of the Russians) that only those who volunteered should be transported home.

After three days an English captain appeared and interrogated me in German. He told me that his mother came from Kárpátalja[141] - I guessed that she was probably Jewish. The interrogation started in a friendly tone, but ended with me becoming indignant. The captain started politicizing, saying that we Hungarians had suppressed the nationalities. I protested that back when we had national minorities, I was still a boy and even later I did not engage in politics. In fact, according to my knowledge, Hungary's only Cardinal and several of the university professors were of Slovak origin and my physics professor, for instance, was Romanian. When I requested to join Regent Horthy (who was in southern Germany), he replied that "Horthy will hang"[142]. I left my written petition with him and departed.

We were still in Lüneburg when on a Sunday we were taken to church. The roof of the church had caved in from bombing. A German Protestant minister led the service. He preached terrible things about the Nazi rule and at the end said that they had referred to Jesus as a "Judenbängel" (Jewish urchin). This sermon, and my anxiety over the fate of my country and family had me break into uncontrolled sobbing. Next to me sat an English escorting officer who held my hand until I quieted down. "My Lord God! What depths have we reached!" he exclaimed.

After a few days we were taken by plane to England. My adjutant and driver were left behind. We landed at Croydon airport and were kept there for two days in a huge prisoner-of-war camp guarded mainly by sailors, with a Navy band that played continuously. Among others, it played the Horst Wessel song several times, amidst great shouts of approval. The mood was good and spirits were high. Apparently the English commander had ordered the song to be played…

---

141 Sub-Carpathia, now part of Russia.
142 In fact, Admiral Horthy was only a witness at the Nuremberg Trials, and was not extradited to Hungary as a war criminal.

I did not know anything about the fate of my family. While I was still at the Lüneburg POW camp, with the permission of the English camp commandant I wrote a British military postcard to my brother-in-law, Kálmán Révész, in America. Unfortunately I did not know his address, only that he was the Executive Secretary of the Verhovay Hungarian insurance company in Pittsburgh, Pennsylvania. (Half a year later I found out that despite the incomplete address, my brother-in-law had received my card and through an American soldier had notified my family, who in the meantime had settled in southern Bavaria in the village of Reichenbach. I had left them in Bayreuth, in the care of the staff of Colonel-General Major).

Following two days at Croydon airport, we were transferred to Windermere (Westmoreland) where we were put in a POW camp which was in an old naval recreational compound. The quarters were crowded and the provisions very weak. I shared a room with four others. My roommates consisted of two Africa Corps generals (veterans of World War I), a one-legged air force general (commander of a fighter division), and another air force general who during the war had been an area commander in Kiev, in the Ukraine, and consequently knew several Hungarian generals personally. His name was Karl Kitzinger[143], and he and I became close friends. He was the one who encouraged me to hold information talks in the camp about Hungary, which I delivered in five parts. After captivity, in both Germany and the USA, he visited us with his wife and daughter.

At the dining room table my companions were former imperial guard officers. Outstanding amongst these was General Kurt von Tippelskirch[144], who wrote the first German military history of the Second World War. During our captivity he was also our

---

143 General der Flieger Karl Kitzinger (1886 - 1962) served as Armed Forces Commander in the Ukraine during 1941 - 1944 before being transferred to France as Military Commander.
144 General der Infanterie Kurt von Tippelskirch (1891 - 1957) had commanded several armies during the war: 4th Army (June 1944), 1st Army in France, 14th Army in Italy, and 21st Army in eastern Germany.

news-media informant. It was characteristic of him that he hated Hitler even in death.

I also got to know General Ferdinand Heim[145], who had been the last German commander of the Boulogne-sur-Mer fortress, where he was taken prisoner during the battles in France following the Allied landing in Normandy. He had been captive for almost a year, and during this time had written his own experiences of Hitler's military leadership in connection with the catastrophe at Stalingrad. I translated Heim's shattering recollections word for word into Hungarian, and they are in my possession to this day. These writings are sincere and true disclosures by a person who participated in the higher German leadership.

Starting in November, the weather turned cold in the Windermere camp. Because of our weight loss on account of being starved (I lost 35 pounds) and, moreover, our shortage of heating fuel, we began to complain. In response our captors allowed us to bring into the camp fallen branches from the nearby forest, and also called for an officer[146] of the Swiss Red Cross to investigate our complaints. Finally, we were promised an improvement in our diet for the approaching Christmas holiday. In the meantime, however, an older general died of a heart attack. The visit from the Red Cross had a surprising result, for after Christmas the camp was transferred to South Wales.

We celebrated Christmas with pudding and English beer (the berries were still in it) and a Luftwaffe general even provided music on a piano. The previous night, when he tried out the piano, he played modern operettas. When he started to play one of the songs from "Csárdáskirálynő[147]", entitled "Far is the forest, far is

---

145 Generalleutnant Ferdinand Heim (1895 - 1977) had commanded a Panzer Corps during the final battle for Stalingrad and had been dismissed from the Army in 1943 for his failure to stop the Russian attack. He was reactivated in August 1944 to command the Boulogne Fortress.
146 Major Fred Bieri.
147 Csárdás Queen, by Imre Kálmán.

the cloud", I began to weep uncontrollably. I was not able to stop - my fate and the fate of my family and country weighed down on me all at once. I still did not know anything about my family. Here I was the only Hungarian and I had no opportunity to speak Hungarian with anyone.

While we were still at Windermere, Colonel-General Gotthard Heinrici[148] joined me several times during our walks. Heinrici had been one of the last commanders of Army Group Vistula, and before that, on the Carpathian front, the German superior commander over the Hungarian 1st Army. He inquired as to the cause for Colonel-General Béla Miklós (commander of the 1st Army) going over to the Russians and wanting to turn his army against the Germans. At that time I was not familiar with the Regent's plans for an armistice and consequently I could not give Heinrici an appropriate answer.

Also at Windermere, a university professor gave German-language lectures on constitutional law. Among other things he mentioned that the English Magna Carta was promulgated in 1215 and thus was the world's oldest constitution. I asked him whether he knew of the Hungarian constitution which had been promulgated by King Endre II. He replied that he did not occupy himself with "dark" Eastern European events. At his next lecture, however, he referred to my question and acknowledged that the Hungarians had received their constitution a mere seven years after the English.

After a day-and-a-half rail trip we arrived at a former American troop camp near the town of Bridgend (South Wales). We were quartered in barracks that had central heating and flowing water. Bridgend, which lies on the northern shore of the Bristol Channel in a park-like, evergreen landscape, had a mild climate. In the spring the meadows were covered with bluebells. Once a week we

---

148   Generaloberst Gotthard Heinrici (1886 - 1971) was dismissed from his command of Army Group Vistula in late April 1945.

were permitted to go on a longer walk. The sea was nearby and the many seagulls created a sense of constant lively activity. We also had a seagull in the camp - it had a broken wing and every morning, when the wind was blowing from the sea, it tried to fly but fell back. The gulls from the sea flew over it every day and dropped fish and clams. This is how it was fed, and it also got scraps from the cooks. On one of our walks, several English newspaper reporters interviewed us. When it was over, we asked the escorting officer why he had permitted the interview. He replied that everything was permitted to the English press.

The group of German generals in this camp were of mixed intellectual capacity. There were three Field Marshals with us: von Rundstedt[149], von Kleist[150], and Sperrle[151] (who was an air force officer). Von Rundstedt was a quiet man who spoke little. He liked music and he whistled much of the time. Liddell Hart[152], the English military historian, had already visited him in Windermere and asked him for clarifications about the final events in France. They discussed these amid amicable wine drinking; Liddell Hart had brought the wine.

Field Marshal von Kleist, a former commander of armored forces, was a lively, open-hearted person with a broad outlook, who chatted with me willingly. He related to me how Hitler had come to power under the presidency of Hindenburg. At the time there had been no other solution, and Hitler had taken a solemn oath in the

---

149 See footnote 49.
150 Generalfeldmarschall Ewald von Kleist (1881 - 1954) was commander of Army Group South Ukraine during March 1943 - March 1944 before being transferred to the reserve. The British handed him over to the Yugoslavs, who in turn delivered him to the Russians. He died in Russian captivity.
151 Generalfeldmarschall Hugo Sperrle (1885 - 1953) was a long-serving commander of Air Fleet (Luftflotte) 3 between February 1939 - October 1944. For four years (1940 - 1944) he was concomitantly C-in-C of the Air Force on the Western Front.
152 Captain Basil Liddell Hart (1895 - 1970) was a leading British military theorist and historian who had retired from the army in 1927. He was knighted in 1966.

Garrison Church of Potsdam, before the Head of State and the whole corps of Generals, that he would respect the constitution.

Field Marshal Sperrle was an infrequent bridge partner of mine, from whom I learned the secrets of the Culbertson system.

There were several generals who had reached their ranks using the political ladder. Among them was one who, for instance, greeted me with "Heil Hitler" even in the spring of 1946; I laughingly asked him whether I should respond with "Heil Szálasi"?

Another of the generals was the former city commandant[153] of Dresden during the time when the U.S. Air Force had carried out the well-known terrible bombing in which, according to him, at least 30,000 people had lost their lives. He had become unhinged…

Yet a third general, who during the war had been the German commander of the island of Cyprus, and in civilian life was the co-owner of a large industrial establishment, spent days trying to convince me to join the Communist party, on the basis of being able to look forward to a glowing future on account of a higher level of culture. He targeted me because rumor had it that Hungary had already turned Communist. In vain, I tried to convince him that he was mistaken; he would not believe me.

To a separate group belonged those officers who, under the leadership of General Student[154], had participated in the conquest of the island of Crete. They were tried by a British military tribunal on the basis of accusations made by the New Zealand government.

---

153 It appears that the author is mistaken in his recollection; the city commandant of Dresden from November 1938 until March 1945 was Generalleutnant Karl Mehnert (1883 - 1957). There is no evidence that General Mehnert was at Bridgend camp, indeed the indications are that he became a prisoner of the Russians at the war's end. General Bor may well have been referring to a subordinate of Generalleutnant Mehnert.

154 Generaloberst Kurt Student (1890 - 1978) was the developer of the German paratroop forces, used to great effect in the capture of Crete.

The indictment consisted of eleven counts and alleged the violation of the Geneva Convention. Five generals were taken from Bridgend to Lüneburg, where the tribunal was hearing the case. One of the generals was Austrian, and it was he who related to me what happened. Of the eleven counts of the indictment, seven were dropped. With regard to the remaining four counts, one of the members of the tribunal, a New Zealand Lieutenant-Colonel who had lost one leg in the war, requested the president to be allowed to give evidence. He testified that he too had participated in the defense of Crete, and of all the charges in the indictment the only one that was true was that the Germans used prisoners of war to dig trenches. As a result the court sentenced General Student, the commander of the Crete operation, to five years in prison. However, the English corps commander pardoned Student on account of his severe head wound. This incident was discussed in the British parliament, where Foreign Minister Bevin commented that against "the international union of generals" nothing could be done.

On one occasion, General Günther Blumentritt[155] held a series of lectures on the events surrounding the battle for Normandy. He had been chief of staff to Field Marshal von Rundstedt at the time of the Allied landings. He recounted von Rundstedt's plan with which Hitler had disagreed. According to the proposed plan, in order to avoid the overwhelming fire power of the Allied naval and air forces, there would have been a withdrawal to the River Seine and from there, in a counterattack, the Allies were to be defeated. At the end of the first lecture von Rundstedt himself spoke a few words in which he emphasized the heroism of the German soldier.

An English general from the War Office visited the camp, and we were permitted to address questions to him. I asked him whether the legal position of "unconditional surrender" applicable to the Germans also applied to me, a Hungarian? He replied that it did not apply to me!

---

155 General der Infanterie Günther Blumentritt (1892 - 1967) commanded the 25th Army and the 1st Parachute Army in the final weeks of the war.

Early in December 1945, General Hasso von Manteuffel[156], General Schimpf[157] and I were escorted to London. Von Manteuffel had commanded one of the attacking Panzer armies during the Ardennes offensive in December 1944. He was a recipient of the Knight's Cross with Oakleaves, Swords and Diamonds. Schimpf had been the commander of a parachute division in the same offensive.

We were quartered in a prison whose commander was an invalid officer of the Guard. Our cell was an empty room with a table and a bench, but no beds and one blanket. As a result of my protestations, they gave me a sheet but nothing to the other two. They took all of our luggage. We could not imagine what the English wanted with us in this jailhouse.

Schimpf discovered that there were several holes in the wall through to the next room. Through one we received a piece of paper with unintelligible writing on it. Our new lodgings did have one advantage: we received better meals. The morning porridge contained fried bacon, and the guard (who was a milk delivery man in the London suburbs) gave us extras.

For two days nothing happened. During this time a supposition of mine was clarified. I had believed that von Manteuffel, with his small stature, was Bavarian and that the large-bodied Schimpf was Prussian. They informed me that the reverse was true; indeed, Frederick the Great, who was Prussian, had also been small of stature.

---

156 General der Panzertruppen Hasso von Manteuffel (1897 - 1978) was a tank expert, who commanded several Panzer armies during the course of the war.
157 Generalleutnant Richard Schimpf (1897 - 1972) was commander of the 3rd Parachute Division during February 1944 - August 1944, when he was wounded. He took over command of the division again in January 1945 until the end of the war. In 1957 he joined the post-war German army (Bundeswehr) as a Generalmajor, retiring in 1962.

On the second day a guard came in excitedly asking whether von Manteuffel had the Knight's Cross with real diamonds? Von Manteuffel pointed to the cross hanging on his neck and to the diamonds above it. The guard examined them closely, and departed in silence. As a result, we were held in greater respect and the guard treated us more amicably.

On the third day I was taken into another hall, where a poorly-dressed and generally seedy-looking civilian introduced himself as C. A. Macartney. He asked me whether I knew him from the Hungarian radio transmission from London? Since I did not know him, he told me that he had been delegated by the War Office to interrogate me in Hungarian. Throughout, he addressed me as "Méltoságos Uram[158]" which indicated to me that he was not Hungarian. Later I found out that he was one of the professors at Edinburgh University, in the Department of International Affairs. He had written several books on the history of Hungary, and was the first one to write about the country's history during the period 1929 - 1945. This work contained numerous errors.

Macartney told me that after the end of the war he had been in Budapest and in several European countries, where he had interviewed Hungarian refugees in connection with the events of 15 October 1944, and he wanted to hear from me about my experiences. Since the war was over, I was willing to answer all of his questions, with the exception of discussing Hungary's war capabilities. For the latter, I would need to obtain a release from official secrecy from the current Hungarian Minister of Defense.

I emphasized that I had never been involved in politics, and the Regent's armistice proclamation had caught me by surprise while I was on an inspection tour in Balatonfüred. Otherwise, I told him everything that I have related earlier in this account. I informed

---

158 "Right Honorable", which was not the correct form of address of an officer of Bor's rank.

Macartney that if Defense Minister János Vörös gave me a written release to reveal official secrets, I would be able to talk about Hungary's war capabilities. He promised that he would obtain the necessary document and adjourned the interrogation. He asked me in the meanwhile to think about the details.

He returned the following day, but since he did not bring with him the Defense Minister's release, my further discussions with him were terminated.

A few years after the 1956 Hungarian revolution against the Communists, the professor was on a tour in America. During this, as a great friend of the Hungarians, he was feted in several cities, including Washington D.C. When we met, he expressed surprise that I had not been put on trial…

Returning to Bridgend, I found that the conditions there were much more humane. At the camp we had religious services every Sunday, with a German Protestant pastor officiating.

Everyone created for himself a vegetable garden and grew lettuce, onions, radishes, and others. We held coffee parties and played bridge in the evenings. Slowly groups formed among the prisoners on the basis of social background and nationality. Only I remained alone. Because my room was next to the reading room, adjoining the rooms of Field Marshals von Rundstedt and von Kleist, I talked frequently with them, particularly with von Kleist.

During the war the German radio introduced its special victory announcements with segments from Franz Liszt's "Les Preludes". During March 1946, the London radio arranged for a week-long Liszt program to commemorate the sixtieth anniversary (1886) of his death, and broadcast selections from his works. Von Rundstedt was quietly reading in the reading room when the Overture from Les Preludes blasted forth from the radio. He snorted like an old war-horse and then admitted that, for a moment, he had expected to hear a victory announcement, but in vain.

Meanwhile I had received news of my family, through the intermediary of an English lady, Miss Edith Kirk, who was the secretary of Sir Harold Webbe, Member of Parliament for the City of London. A friend of my brother-in-law (in America) had visited this lady and sent a message through her that my wife and son were in Reichenbach (Germany) and they knew that I was in English captivity. In Germany there are five cities named Reichenbach - I was unable to guess in which one they were located. I exchanged several letters with Edith Kirk, but was unable to find out more from her either.

XIII. Release and life in Germany

In August 1946, I was notified that I should prepare for repatriation. Although I had reported that I did not wish to return to Hungary, I was not certain that I would not forcibly be sent home. I prepared myself for an escape attempt on the way, if it became necessary, because I had not received an answer to my request to go to Germany. On 20 August, accompanied by a British sergeant, I was taken to London Docks where I embarked on a ship.

Before I embarked, a Hungarian lady stopped me and identified herself as an employee of the Hungarian temporary diplomatic representation. She asked me whether I wanted to return home, and I replied that I did not. "You should not go," she said, "but did you report your intentions to the military authorities?". I replied in the affirmative, adding that I had not yet received an answer. "Then report it again every place where they take you!" she said. She added that the temporary chargé d'affaires, Consul Bede, sent his greetings, and with this we parted.

I was shown to a cabin, where I set myself up in comfort. At seven in the morning - we were already at sea - a steward woke me up with a cup of tea with milk. As I stepped out of the cabin, I bumped into some Hungarian artillery men who greeted me with great joy and asked me whether I had already had breakfast. I told them that I had not, so they led me to the mess hall where they served me a full breakfast. On the rest of the trip I conversed amicably with the officers.

We arrived at Antwerp, where an English officer came for me and took me in his car to a fort where the English were serving as guards. They put me up in a cold cell, where a fire had to be lit for heat, and invited me for lunch at the officers' mess. Here a major approached with about six other officers. He introduced me to his officers and seated me next to him. During lunch, with my poor

English I related to the major that I did not want to go to Hungary, where I would fall into Russian captivity, and that my family was in southern Germany, which is where I would like to go. He promised that he would report this to the British Headquarters Command, and I should await the decision.

Next day another major and a second officer came for me. The major spoke perfect German and addressing me as "Herr Feldmarschalleutnant" asked me what I desired. I told him what I wanted and when I said that I did not want to fall into Russian captivity, his companion remarked that this was very understandable. While we were having coffee, they related that the behavior of the Russians in Berlin was "unspeakably shocking".

The major then put me in his jeep and took me to a POW camp near Zeebrugge, where I was to await the decision regarding my destination. This camp was full of sailors and army officers who were crawling around on the verge of death. All around was a swamp and a canal flowed through the middle of the camp, full of croaking frogs which the prisoners attempted to catch. We were quartered in small, tin-roofed storage huts which in the summertime were unbearably hot during the day but pleasantly cool in the night.

Here I made the acquaintance of German General Hermann Harrendorf[159], who as a division commander during the last phases of the war had fought in western Hungary. He spoke with enthusiasm about the country, and we became good friends. The provisioning at this camp was abominably weak, but Harrendorf's wife sent him a little potato powder and fat from which potato cakes could be fried. He shared this with me several times.

As the time that I had to wait in this place grew longer, I complained about the unspeakable conditions to Edith Kirk, in a secret letter. The letter had several results: first a sergeant came and

---

159 Generalmajor Hermann Harrendorf (1896 - 1966) commanded the 96th Infantry Division between December 1944 and May 1945.

took several photographs of me; then officers of the Counter Intelligence Corps interrogated me, and finally the camp commandant was replaced.

At last a decision arrived from the British Headquarters, or rather, from the occupation headquarters of the U.S. army which gave a negative answer that did not permit my release into their zone. The new camp commandant informed me of this with the comment that he could release me to any place under British occupation. He told me that I should think this over and let him know where I wished to be released. I asked the lieutenant-colonel for time to consider and returned to my quarters. There I related my situation to Harrendorf. He immediately offered his home in Hamburg as an address, and said that he would write to his wife for her to give me shelter.

Accordingly, I requested my release to Hamburg. A sergeant, who in peacetime had graduated from the conservatory of music in Berlin, took me by military train to Munster Lager (about 38 miles south of Hamburg) where my release took place. I traveled to Hamburg by night train, arriving in the morning, where I took a streetcar to Altona, Elbchaussee 204. Mrs. Harrendorf received me sadly, because her husband had not come with me.

I found out that at the Town Hall was the Military Office where I could get food ration cards and a rail ticket to travel to Bavaria. I went there and they released me, without any objections, to go to Reichenbach as a discharged soldier. I telegraphed my wife to let her know where I was, and a couple of days later my son arrived for the purpose of escorting me to Reichenbach. He brought with him food and cigarettes which could be utilized for paying any bribes along the way.

The Harrendorf house, a pretty villa-like building, lay on the north shore of the River Elbe, with a large orchard on the river side of the building. During my year-and-a-half of captivity, I had not eaten any fruit. Also, having lost a lot of weight and in my weakened state, even my walk was unsteady. Mrs. Harrendorf complained that she had no-one to pick her pears and apples that were ripe, and asked me to pick as much for myself as I could. I picked and ate the fruit for three days and started to feel much better.

Our train started from the station in Altona, but we had to be there hours earlier to get space on it. Even then, my son had to climb through a window with the luggage and could secure only one seat.

We traveled more than 26 hours before we reached Munich. During the night a girl stole packs of cigarettes from my son's pocket. From Munich we went by local train through Kempten to Langenwang, which was the rail stop for Reichenbach. From the station we had to hike over a mile to Reichenbach. Reichenbach was a dairy-farming village with about 30 houses, situated at an altitude of about 3,300 feet. It had a small mountain hotel in which eight Hungarian families were housed, together with a doll factory that they had founded. These Hungarians were the District Commander's favorites because they supported themselves with their own work and, unlike the other refugees, did not require assistance. Moreover, they even paid for their rent at the hotel.

In the middle of September 1946, I arrived at the hotel where my family lived. The mayor (a local merchant) protested against my settling here - I was supposed to have gone to a camp first. The District Commander, however, in view of the fact that I had living quarters and work, permitted me to stay. I joined the workforce of the doll factory. I worked 10 hours every day; on odd days I sewed body forms for dolls, on even days I painted wooden plates with Hungarian folk designs.

For a while my son went to school in Oberstdorf, and then he worked at the American garrison in Sonthofen as a civilian employee. In 1947 I took him to Passau to a Hungarian school, located in a camp, where he matriculated. In late 1947 he then went to London, with assistance from my American brother-in-law, and with the help of Edith Kirk he matriculated in English. From there, my brother-in-law brought him to the United States as a student, where in Pittsburgh (Pennsylvania) he completed his university studies.

In 1948 the German monetary system was changed. The doll factory did not fare badly from the currency reform, however, its future became uncertain because it could not compete, as regards quality, with the German factories. For this reason, I proposed that we change to the production of embroidered women's dresses. My proposal was rejected by a majority, therefore I left the factory and entered American service. In Sonthofen I obtained a civilian office job.

The commandant of the American garrison (made up of an artillery regiment) needed civilian support personnel. The hiring of these was handled by a civilian personnel division, and I was employed in this division. My chief was a Department of the Army civilian named Zoche. He gave the impression of being a wild man, but fundamentally he was a kind-hearted person, of German descent. He was particularly well-disposed towards Hungarian officers, and chatted with me many times. When the Korean War broke out he immediately questioned me as to my opinion. When I found out that the U.S.A. needed about a month to ship a larger force over there, I assured him that - with a two-sided encirclement - attacking the advancing enemy from the rear, a decision in favor of the Americans could be gained within a few months. We made a bet and General MacArthur, outflanking from only one side, won my bet for me.

My pay was sufficient for my family's needs, but the daily travel (including the walk into Sonthofen) had me on my feet 14 hours a day. We needed to move, so we found a room, with the use of a bathroom and kitchen, in a suburb of Sonthofen with Mrs. Lechner, a widow who also had a little son - Hanzi. I walked from here to the City Hall, where I worked, until 1950. I would have my lunch there in a mess hall maintained by the Americans.

It was at this time that my wife, having lived through all the stresses, homelessness, and temporary loss of her son, had a serious nervous breakdown. First she was treated at home, but later she spent over a month in a hospital in Oberstdorf, but she showed no improvement.

In 1950, in connection with a major reorganization, my division was transferred to the Augsburg garrison, and I was to accompany it. I had my wife admitted to the city hospital of Augsburg, but this proved to be a bad choice, for instead of improving she turned much worse, and in the end my wife had to be taken to a sanatorium. This was in a smallish town, about 80 miles northwest of Augsburg, not far from Stuttgart. The autobahn was covered in ice and many cars had overturned. An American vehicle had skidded so badly that it flipped over on its top. During the entire trip to the sanatorium I was very concerned that, although we were travelling in a heavy ambulance, we too would overturn. In the end we arrived in one piece and were received very kindly. My wife regained her health in the sanatorium.

My brother-in-law was actively promoting our emigration to the United States, particularly after he had arranged for my son to go to London. While still at Reichenbach we received a summons to go to Augsburg to process our emigration. This processing lasted a whole month and at the end of it we were not given permission to emigrate on the grounds that I, as a general officer, would have had the means to influence the politics of my government. I protested and requested the central office in Geneva to make known the real reason why our application had been denied. In the meantime, we moved to Sonthofen, where we received the reply.

It stated that it was the Szálasi government that had promoted me (to Lieutenant-Field Marshal) and had entrusted me with a high office. In response to this I renounced my wish to emigrate and informed the central office that the statement was a malicious lie, because I had been promoted and appointed to high office by the Regent himself, on 1 September 1944. I demanded that they delete the false assertions from my interrogation documents forthwith. However, my brother-in-law continued to intervene on my behalf. The American-Hungarian Association sent Artur Dobozy, its empowered emissary, to investigate certain cases. Dobozy put my particular case in order, helped by an order by the Western Powers that reorganized the refugee system. Consequently, I was called in again to the emigration center in Augsburg. I awaited the final steps of the process in my office, since by then my place of employment was in Augsburg.

Meanwhile, the Augsburg Housing Board alloted me an abandoned two-room apartment into which my wife and I moved. Before this, I had lived in a furnished room at Branderstrasse 34, owned by Frau Legath. Augsburg is a city with a tremendous historical past and tradition, situated in southern Germany (Bavaria). It had even played a role in Hungarian history: in the 10th Century, a large Magyar force suffered a heavy defeat on the nearby Lechfeld plain which put an end to further adventurous expeditions. In the Middle Ages, the city was made famous by the large spinning and weaving factory of the Fuggers. During the Reformation, events took place here the results of which are still visible. For instance, the good business-minded citizens amicably agreed upon the division of churches. The Ulrich Cathedral remained Catholic, while the convent church - built right next to the cathedral - was changed to Lutheran. The original Catholic church in the fortress, with beautiful paintings depicting events of church history on the inner walls, became Lutheran, while the Catholics built another church for themselves in the same courtyard. Unfortunately, the center of the city - along with several monuments - had been totally bombed out during the war. Only sections of the old fortress walls are still standing today. Also preserved are the canals, created by diverting the River Lech, that supplied motive power to craft shops in the city as well as to the linen factory.

By the end of June 1951 we were finally notified to prepare for emigration. We were transported by rail to the Bremerhaven assembly camp, where we had to wait for about four weeks until embarkation. Because everyone had to accept some type of work assignment, I volunteered to be an English language instructor. I taught two hours every day. The mentality of the pupils was quite low, but the teaching was not much better…

On 28 July we finally embarked and departed. Our 25th wedding anniversary (30 July) found us at sea. We could not celebrate it, however, because I became so seasick for three or four days that I could not even get out of bed. When we reached the Gulf Stream a terrible storm hit us. An old Jewish lady died, and was put on ice until our arrival in New York.

XIV. Emigration to the USA

On 3 August the Statue of Liberty in New York harbor finally appeared on the horizon. We had arrived. It took another day to go through another screening check before we were allowed to set foot on shore. My brother-in-law was waiting for us below, with his whole family and a strange young man in the background, who turned out to be our son, Jenci. After leaving our large luggage with a transport agency, we settled in a huge hotel near the Pennsylvania Railroad Station. Everything we saw and experienced seemed to be unearthly luxury. Kálmán took us to Radio City Music Hall where, in a three-hour-long program we saw the musical "Showboat" along with some concert pieces. Then we went to supper where it struck me as unusual that everybody was first served a glass of fresh water. The city was dazzlingly illuminated, and the ground and sky were covered with blinding advertisements. When I commented on this luxury, I was told that with increased consumption more money circulates, with the result of more personal income for everyone.

Next evening we flew to the airport of Pittsburgh (Pennsylvania) where a friend of my brother-in-law Kálmán awaited us with Kálmán's automobile and drove us to Kálmán's house in a ride that took more than an hour.

Kálmán's house was situated in the Mount Lebanon suburb of Pittsburgh. It was a small family home with a garage and basement, modernly furnished and with a garden-city type of surrounding. The neighbor's yard had fruit trees full with ripe fruit to which nobody paid any attention. The neighbors were vacationing.

Immediately I had to look for a job. Kálmán introduced me to one of the directors of the Mellon Bank with whom the Verhovay Insurance Company (Kálmán's firm) did business. (Of the Mellon Bank building and the gothic skyscraper building of the University of Pittsburgh, it was said that the latter was the "Cathedral of Learning" while the former was the "Cathedral of Earning"). The director recommended me to the Gulf Company, which was engaged in the distribution of oil products throughout the country, but we determined that I did not possess appropriate experience. I was then offered a job as an elevator operator in the ALCOA building, but I did not accept.

I had been looking for a job in vain for nearly two weeks when our nieces, who were living in Richmond (Virginia) invited us to visit them, saying that there would be an appropriate job for me there. I traveled to Richmond through Washington, a six hour trip by bus. My nieces Magda and Ruth were waiting for me there. They lived on Hanover Avenue with a friend of theirs, near the Boulevard. It was the house of an elderly couple who lived on the first floor. The husband of Magda's co-worker worked in a civil engineering office as a surveyor, and through him I obtained a job there as a draftsman. The name of the company was La Prade Civil Engineering Company.

My starting salary was $35 per week, but my job lasted only three months before I changed to an outside surveying job. Mr. Bud Weiser, who was in charge of the outside work, accepted me into his team as the fourth member. Weiser was a surveyor by profession, but had an aptitude for a lot of other things. He was the most original person that fate had ever let me meet. He was gaunt, skin and bone, very lively, the Uncle Sam-type appearance without the beard much like you see depicted in cartoons. Moreover, he was cultured - he recited poems by Dante and knew works by Edgar Allan Poe by heart, as well as popular ballads. Our jobs took us far from Richmond, traveling for hours by car until we reached our job site, during which Mr. Weiser talked about his own life and about anything else that came to his mind. He was the person who introduced me to American life!

It was about this time that General MacArthur wound up the Korean War victoriously. The general, however, planned to follow up his victory with a further advance into North Korea. The political leadership protested against such a course of action, and to close the debate President Truman relieved MacArthur of his command. The process of relieving him was done so awkwardly that I became indignant and told Mr. Weiser that such a thing would not happen in Europe. To kick out, like a servant, a national hero who had won two wars for the country was just unheard of. Weiser commented that there was a little ditty about this, "MacArthur had a little horse whose face is very human, but when it turns the other way it looks like Harry Truman…". "Well," I said, "this is not a very nice comment on the head of state". Mr. Weiser responded, "But with this, everybody gets what he deserves. Don't let it bother you Mr. Bor".

All winter and spring we worked in the woods along the James River. Weiser had an old Ford automobile which had run over 200,000 miles and, under the back seat, it was so full of holes that my colleagues assured me that we would fall through it one day. I, however, stuck it out faithfully with him until one day on the open highway, the motor broke down completely - the oil had run out. The junkyard bought it for five dollars.

During lunch breaks we shot at targets with a .22-caliber pistol that Weiser secretly brought with him every day. He was a great collector of old pistols. He had a pistol from 1830 for which he made the ammunition himself, using black powder. On a rainy Sunday afternoon he invited me to a thicket near his home to target shoot with his various weapons. It happened here that my hearing, well preserved through two world wars, became impaired. He fired one of his blunderbusses near my right ear and I remained deaf on that side for a month.

We met many hunters in the autumn woods. Their dogs chased the game with no control from their masters. Several times we came across a white buck. Nobody bothered him, only the dogs chased him. Hunters' superstition…

We frequently came across snakes in the swampy sections of the woods. Weiser became enraged every time we met a snake - he chased it with an axe until he executed it. It did not matter whether the snake was poisonous or not.

Late in the spring the firm received an assignment for a highway. For this, everone had to regroup under the direction of another engineer. On the highway there was a great deal of traffic toward Norfolk and in the opposite direction. The road traversed many streams and marshes. It was very hard work and for the first time I felt that I could not physically cope with the tempo. Although my income was sometimes as high as $50 per week, I had to stop the outside work. I wrote to my brother-in-law that he should try to get me an inside job someplace else. This is how I ended up in Washington at the Airsurvey Corporation.

During our stay in Richmond, our son was also there as a seminary student. We rarely saw him because he was very busy. In the summer, however, he surprised us with an announcement that he intended to leave the seminary and get married. Because he had only a student's visa he had to clarify his citizenship-residency status. To this end he had himself drafted, for two years of service in the army. Beforehand, he brought his future wife for an introducion.

In July 1952 I came to Washington D.C. to the Airsurvey Corporation, to introduce myself, and within a few weeks I was hired. Because as a former artillery officer I knew trigonometry and calculating machines, I joined the company as an engineer.

The company made maps from aerial photographs, which were usually used in the construction of roads and high-tension transmission lines. The aerial photographs needed to be placed into the national triangulation system. For this, ground measurements were needed, the points of which were marked on the photographs. I had to calculate the results of the ground measurements and the positioning of the photographs into the national system. On account of the fact that I had not dealt with photogrammetry before, I completed three semesters of training and acquired the necessary credits. (I had to discontinue one semester because of illness). I was in this job for three years. We mapped in Pennsylvania, Alabama and in the northern part of Minnesota, and we also worked as a sub-contractor for the Army Map Service on some of their airfields in Spain.

The owners of the Airsurvey Corporation were members of the Christian Science Church and therefore did not provide health insurance for their employees. I found this out when I had to undergo an operation for gallstones. I was unable to work for four months. The company paid for two weeks of regular leave and two weeks of sick leave, and, since my private insurance was small, I had to pay the hospital costs in installments for two years.

In 1955, Congress did not vote into law the bill for national highway construction on which our company was very much counting. Therefore, because of the lack of work, they terminated about twenty employees and I was among them. I had to look for a new position. Along with several other fellow workers, I found a job with the Airways Engineering Corporation, a company that specialized in the expansion and construction of airfields. Here I learned to do calculations that involved the planning of earth excavations and the scheme of access roads to airports.

Before I started working for Airways Engineering Corporation, I accepted work (for about twenty days) at Johnson & Associates in Arlington. My experience here with respect to my co-workers was depressing. My predecessor, for instance, made an error of several feet in the calculations to position a building on a corner lot; as a result the foundation had to be moved at a cost of about $2,000.

I worked at Airways Engineering Corporation from September 1955 to December 1956. During this time, on 9 October 1956, we became United States citizens. Between 23 October - 4 November, the Hungarian revolution took place, which the Russians drowned in blood.

In the second half of December, being again unemployed, I went to Camp Killmer to help the deputation from the American-Hungarian Association with the reception and placing into jobs of the mulitude of Hungarian refugees. Here I had a number of interesting meetings.

Among others, I met my successor as Chief of the Main Material Group in the Hungarian Defense Ministry, former General Miklós Nagyőszy[160], who had been set free after several years of imprisonment. Initially I was not sure who I was looking at - he came toward me in the company of his wife and a pipe-smoking farmer. I had a notion that I knew him and asked him who he was. He identified himself to me. To my knowledge he had a wife and family who, after eleven years of separation, where waiting for him here in America. What would happen to the second wife? He divorced the first wife, and the problem was solved.

Between January and April 1957, chief engineer John Martin of Keystone Mapping invited me to be his deputy. The company was a subsidiary of the York (Pennsylvania) firm. Here again I ran into inexperienced co-workers as a result of which, on one occasion, I had to go to York for two weeks to make some measurements and calculations.

On 8 April 1957, I was finally called to the Army Map Service for a position as a cartographer. I had submitted my application there immediately upon receiving my citizenship and it had taken this long to be processed[161]. My acceptance was important because I was already 62 years old and in three years I would have to retire from a civilian job. In the government job, I could serve until I was seventy-five.

---

160   Lieutenant-Field Marshal Miklós Nagyőszy (1896 - 1968) was a former Corps commander who took over Bureau III of the Defense Ministry in December 1944. After the war he was jailed by the Communist regime, but was released in 1953. He escaped Hungary during the 1956 Revolution.

161   The author's old acquaintance from the end-of-war days in Germany, Colonel Szilárd Zigury, was already employed there, and helped a great deal in expediting the application.

I had finally entered a sphere of activity for which my earlier career provided a good basis. I was knowledgeable in all areas of the work to be done. The scope of the Army Map Service (later renamed Army Topographic Command) is the whole world, in fact, not just the Earth, but also beyond the Earth. It studies the mapping of all the countries of each of the continents; it also advises these countries or participates in their mapping efforts. The globe is covered with a grid system of measured points which form the basis of maps. Individual systems of the various nations, or the maps resulting from the work of the Map Service's own experts, are melded into a universal system which is updated as new data becomes available.

The Army Map Service's work beyond the globe is multi-faceted. It maps the earth-facing surface of the moon with the aid of photogrammetry. The landing of the astronauts on the moon was directed with the aid of these maps. Satellites circling the moon were used to reconnoiter the unseen parts of the moon. Finally, again with the use of photogrammetry, the Service made generalized maps of Mars. The extraterrestrial work also includes triangulation with the use of artificial satellites, for the purpose of terrestrial measurements.

My sphere of work was demarcated as Western Europe. This was the mission of a separate division which was part of the Foreign Control Group (Foreign Networks). Initially we worked on the preparation of a network for the contemporary mapping of the successor countries of the Austro-Hungarian Empire (including Hungary). Later we did the same for Germany, Italy and Spain. Subsequently, I took over the uniform altitude determination inventory of Western Europe.

My division chief was Edgar A. Roell and his deputy was Walter Megaw. We became very good friends and they appreciated me as a person as well as for my work. They were my bridge partners on many occasions.

As with all military organizations, ours was reorganized several times. Today, my old division also encompasses Eastern Europe as well as Northern Asia. The leaders have also changed.

On 1 August 1970, one month before my 75th birthday, I retired. After a long and experience-packed life, I had earned a deserved rest. The good Lord led me through many dangers and difficulties, and I owe Him my eternal gratitude. I owe Him eternal gratitude for having blessed me with a faithful wife who stood by me through everything, and that through my son's marriage I was blessed with four grandsons who will carry on the family tradition and will be strong members of the Family of Man.

List of Sources

The following is a list of primary sources used in the compilation of the footnotes:

Bölöny, József. *Magyarország Kormányai, 1848 - 1975.* Budapest: Akadémia Kiadó, 1978.

Bradley, D./Hildebrand, K./Rövekamp, M. *Die Generale des Heeres 1921 - 1945, Band I - VI.* Osnabrück: Biblio Verlag, 1993-2002.

Hildebrand, K. F. *Die Generale der Deutschen Luftwaffe 1935 - 1945, Band I - III.* Osnabrück: Biblio Verlag, 1990-1992.

Hungarian Historical Research Society. *A Magyar Királyi Honvédség és Csendörség Rangsorolása 1944 (I. - III. kötet).* Universe Publishing Company, 1976.

Keilig, Wolf. *Die Generale des Heeres.* Friedberg: Podzun-Pallas-Verlag, 1983.

Kursietis, Andris. *The Hungarian Army & Its Leadership in World War II.* Bayside: Axis Europa Books & Magazines, 1999.

Kursietis, Andris. *The Royal Hungarian Armed Forces 1919 - 1945.* Milwaukee: ARK Publications Co., 1994-1997.

Kursietis, Andris. *The Wehrmacht at War 1939 - 1945.* Soesterberg: Aspekt, 1999.

Szakály, Sándor. *A Magyar Katonai Felsö Vezetés.* Budapest: Ister, 2001.